D1436657

WHAT HAPPENED TO THE HIPPY MAN?

Hijack hostage survivor

Mike Thexton

Lanista
PARTNERS

LONDON

First published in Great Britain in 2006 by
LANISTA PARTNERS LTD

Hippyman Publishing
PO Box 778
RICHMOND
TW9 3XA
United Kingdom

www.hippyman.com

ISBN 0-9553185-0-5

13-digit ISBN 978-0-9553185-0-4

A catalogue record for this book is available from the British Library.

Typeset in Times New Roman

Printed and bound in Great Britain by

The Alden Press, Oxford

For the heroines of PA 073: Neerja, Sunshine and all the others

For those who died

Rajesh N. Kumar, 29, USA
Surendra Manubhai Patel, 50, USA
Kuverben Patel, 81, India (Rajesh Kumar's grandmother)
Syed Nesar Ahmad, 43, Pakistan
Kala Singh, 36, India
Imran Rizvi, 17, Pakistan
Seetharamiah Krishnaswamy, 61, India
Trupti Dalal, 28, India
Meherjee Minocher Kharas, 28, Pakistan
Jose Alvarez Lamar Nunez, 57, Mexico
Ricardo Munoz Rosales, 28, Mexico
Neerja Bhanot, 23, India
Ganapathi Thanikaimoni, 48, India
Boby Thomachen Mulloor, 7, India
Thomachen Thomas Mulloor, 30, India (Boby's father)
Aleyamma Scaria Nagatholy, 39, India
Ramakant Ramakrishna Naik, 55, India
Rupal Desai, 26, India
Kodiyatu K. Kurian, 25, India

Acknowledgements

There are too many people who have helped with this to thank them all. Thanks to Greg Child for providing some pictures of Pete and letting me borrow some of his writing. Thanks to Sunshine, whose account provided some of the most important parts that I didn't see myself. Thanks to John, the Aviation Security Advisor who thought the tale worth telling in a book. Thanks to Jane for the final proofreading. And thanks to Neil, the Evil Publisher, for his belief in the project, as well as his editing and improving of the text.

I am also grateful to the many survivors, witnesses and others connected to the story who have helped or given permission for the use of words and pictures – among them Ranee, Viraf, Aneesh, Prabhat and Gregg. Thanks also to those members of the cabin crew who wished the book well but preferred to be left out of it.

Finally, thanks to my wife Kathy, who had to put up with a lot while I was writing it.

Contents

Illustrations

FOREWORD AND FOREWARNING

I am going to tell a true story of murder and mayhem. Real people are killed and maimed, and yet the comedy of the absurd runs through it. That may seem in bad taste, but there is some grim humour in the bleakest situations. Not that they tend to be so funny at the time. It is easier to look on the light side knowing the outcome. I survived. This won't be a whodunit, nor a did-he-get-out-of-it. However, I wasn't laughing in the face of danger on the day itself.

I have told this story to an audience many times over the years, but I have not written it down in this way before. I think it may be easier to make gallows humour work 'live'. We'll see.

The best reason for including jokes is that without a bit of humour this story is plain nasty – it's no fun to tell, and not much fun for an audience to hear or for you to read. Lightening it up balances the death and destruction with the strength of human nature to cope. I hope that it will not diminish the tragedy – but will make it manageable. I do not intend any disrespect to those who died, or who lost someone.

Of course, that raises the question: why tell the story at all? If it's that unpleasant to tell and to read, perhaps it should be left alone. It's certainly not a new story, not a hot scoop (or so I thought until recently). However, it is a good story: people have told me so over the years, and I have seen the expression on their faces while they hear it. It is a tale with villains and with heroes – mainly, in fact, with heroines. Their story deserves telling.

Another reason for writing it down now is that it seems still to be very relevant. We are in the middle of a war on terrorism that started with a series of aircraft hijackings. The world seems to become a more dangerous place as this war goes on. That may be a real, or merely a perceived, increase in danger – but there are lessons in this story about dealing with terror, and more people might need to know them.

A final and startling reason for telling the story now is one that occurred only in the middle of checking the final draft of this book. In April 2006, US lawyers launched a $10 billion class action against

Colonel Gadaffy and Libya – the man and state they believe were behind it all. Maybe this is a whodunit after all.

I will also include some opinions. When I started writing, I thought that the facts at least would be easy and relatively uncontroversial: I was there, no-one else could argue much about the facts. Even the facts turn out to be more slippery than I had thought, and I have learned new and significant details of a story I believed I had been retelling accurately for nineteen years. If even the facts can be elusive, opinions are downright dangerous: people can get very stirred up about opinions, particularly where Palestinian terrorism is concerned. But everyone seems to have opinions. Mine come from the perspective that the wrong end of a Kalashnikov gives you, and I think I'm entitled to them. If you don't agree with them, please try not to be outraged. They're just opinions, and I have not the slightest influence in the world.

There are other people in this story, but I will not name them, except when it is absolutely necessary. Apart from the hijackers, they did not choose to be involved in the event, and I will not presume that they want to be involved in my telling of the story. I will relate the facts as they concerned me – not from a desire to exclude the others, but just to concentrate on what I know and what I can tell best. There are just a few points where I have borrowed someone else's story, when my own experience would not be enough to get across what it was like to be on the inside of a hijacked plane. I hope that those people won't mind me telling a little of what they went through.

A WALK IN THE VALLEY OF THE SHADOW

On 5 September 1986, five Palestinian terrorists, members of the Abu Nidal Organisation, seized a Pan Am jumbo jet at Karachi airport, Pakistan. Four stormed the plane as it stood on the runway; the fifth, the mastermind, stayed behind outside the airport. In the initial confusion, the flight crew escaped, and the aircraft became a ground-based stronghold.

Early on, they shot a passenger and threw his body out to show they meant business. They picked out another and held him at the front under threat of execution to emphasise their demands.

After about sixteen hours, the auxiliary power unit – running the jumbo's electrical systems while on the ground – failed, and the inside of the plane became dark. The terrorists opened fire on the passengers with automatic weapons and threw hand-grenades into the cabins, killing another nineteen and injuring a hundred. The passengers and cabin crew – those who still could move – opened the emergency exits and ran away.

This is my story of that day, and afterwards.

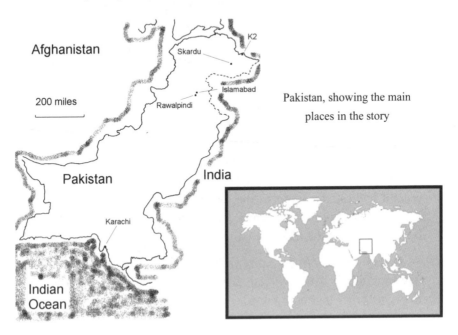

Pakistan, showing the main places in the story

Storyboard

In a Hollywood disaster film, you always get a 30 second introduction to each of the main characters – the ones we are supposed to care about – so you know that this man is on his way to sort out his failing marriage; this woman has a terminal illness; that man is on the point of losing his job. In real life, most of the people in such a situation are probably on a routine journey. However, everything that brought them there will affect how they react to the crisis. You can't predict exactly how they will behave based on how they got there, but it will surely have an effect. The cameo background may be a simplistic device in a film, but the principle is surprisingly important in the real world. So I will give you the Hollywood vignette. As I'm the main character, I'll even give myself more than 30 seconds. The film rights are available as long as I'm played by someone good-looking.

It all begins with my older brother, Pete. He was a mountaineer and a doctor, in that order. He progressed from hill-walking on family holidays, to rock-climbing at boarding school, to Alpine trips from medical school, to Himalayan expeditions in the gaps between junior doctor appointments. The gaps were extensive. While I was at university, he came to give a slide show to the climbing club. The president and officers of the climbing club, demigods at college, obviously regarded him as the full deity. While I started my training as an accountant, he was off climbing Everest in winter (more accurately, *not* climbing Everest in winter, but he broke some ribs trying).

In May 1983, he went on an expedition to northern Pakistan which aimed to ascend three peaks: Lobsang Spire, an unclimbed rock pinnacle 18,742 feet high (5,713 metres); Broad Peak, considered an easy ascent by the hardest mountaineers, but still the twelfth highest mountain in the world at 26,400 feet (8,047 metres); and K2, the second highest mountain in the world at 28,250 feet (8,611 metres). It's a harder climb than Everest, and getting to the top without bottled oxygen is one of the toughest mountaineering challenges.

Pete climbed Lobsang Spire with Doug Scott and Greg Child, a six-day rock climb that involved sleeping on "portaledges" – something like a stretcher tied onto the near-vertical rock face. They reached the top on 13 June, the last pitch requiring Greg to drill tiny holes in the featureless rock to take the smallest of hooks for the climbers to pull up on.

The Spire was just a warming-up exercise, and so was Broad Peak – the real target was K2. The ascent of Broad Peak was part of the process of acclimatisation to high altitude. Base camp for the big mountains was three days further on from the Spire. The expedition split up into pairs to climb Broad Peak – Pete and Greg had formed a strong friendship, even though they had not met before the expedition, and they were the fourth pair of five. The ascent started on 25 June, and on the morning of 28 June they were at the high camp ready to go for the summit, about 24,500 feet up (7,450 metres). At that level, you are in the upper half of the troposphere. Oxygen is so short that you are dying slowly every second you stay. Sleeping brings little rest. A climber needs to get up and down as fast as possible.

Greg tells how that morning Pete woke up still dreaming, and asked him, "What about this rope then?"

"Rope? Our rope is in the pack."

"Noooo, not that rope."

"Then what rope?"

"The rope we're all tied into."

"We're not tied in, Pete, we're in the tent, Camp Four, Broad Peak."

"Noooo, you don't understand. It's the rope that all of us are tied to."

Greg couldn't get an explanation before Pete woke up properly and the moment passed.

They set off for the summit and reached the north summit at about 1.30pm. The true summit is only 18 feet higher, but is half an hour away – one of the highest ridge walks in the world. At this point, Greg started to be seriously worried about his ability to go on: he was used to the normal blinding headache that comes with high altitude, but he started blacking out for moments at a time, coming back to consciousness a few paces further on. He thought he might easily step off the ridge. He could be having a stroke, or suffering the first symptoms of cerebral oedema, in which fluid leaks into the brain cavity and leads to blindness, unconsciousness, death.

They talked it over. Pete was keen on summits, and he reminded Greg that he had "murdered the impossible" with his drill on Lobsang Spire in order to sit on the top. But he recognised that Greg couldn't go on. When Greg suggested that he would wait for Pete to go to the summit and return, Pete refused: "We stay together."

So they started down, Greg gradually feeling better as they went. But Pete started to feel worse. His breathing became difficult, he slowed down to a crawl. He could not see where he was going. Greg had to lift, lower, heave him down through the rest of daylight and into the dark. It is hard to imagine what they both went through in that descent, and I don't want to try. Even after 23 years, thinking about it too directly can reduce me to tears. I don't know why – it's all a long time ago. I have to look away, even in my mind's eye.

At 2.00am on 29 June, 22 hours after they set out, they reached the high camp again. Don Whillans was there with a high altitude porter, Gohar Shah. They made Pete comfortable, and Greg collapsed into an exhausted sleep. Two hours later, at dawn, Pete seemed to wake and ask Gohar for a drink of water. But he did not take any from the mug that was offered. He was dead. Pulmonary oedema, the leaking of fluid into the lungs, had effectively drowned him.

He is buried there, in a crevasse high on Broad Peak. Greg had carried him alive as far as he could, but it was not possible to bring down his body.

The news took two weeks to reach us, during which time I took my final accountancy exams, got drunk to celebrate, and went back to work after the long study leave period, with no idea of the message of grief that was walking out of the mountains with Greg and Don. They reached a phone on 14 July, and the message came by way of Doug Scott's wife and my parents.

Pete was just 30, six years older than me. I was shattered. The prospect of a career in accountancy lost much of its allure, and I left my job to work as a freelance lecturer. This gave me the freedom to do more interesting things. Now that my brother wasn't around to provide the excitement in my life by proxy, I thought I would have to work harder at it. One of my big ideas was to write books (not as easy as it looks, I found – none published before this one, and I'm still teaching accountants).

After Pete died, it was my ambition to go to the foot of Broad Peak to say goodbye. I knew I would not be able to go to the place itself – even if it could be found – but I could at least stand at the bottom of the mountain and recite some indifferent poetry I had written. He would have been very surprised to see me there, and probably fairly scornful of the verse.

I am no more a climber than I am a poet, and this was a nice, safe ambition that was unlikely to come to anything. I read books and saw television programmes about these places, and they looked mighty dangerous to me.

Then, in 1985, some students from the climbing club at St. Mary's Hospital in Paddington, the medical school where he trained, told my family that they wanted to organise an expedition in Pete's honour. They went to Kenya to do some climbing and to research aspects of altitude sickness. The expedition was a success, and afterwards the leaders hatched a more ambitious plan for 1986. They would go to the Karakoram Himalaya in Pakistan, make a first ascent of an unclimbed route on Pete's last successful peak – Lobsang Spire – and do more research.

They asked me to go along as the Base Camp Manager. I took a deep breath, and realised that I would have to fulfil my daydream. I interpreted the role they offered as meaning that I would Manage to Get to Base Camp, and as

7

long as I wouldn't have to do anything beyond that, I was prepared to take the job.

ST. MARY'S HOSPITAL
MOUNTAINEERING CLUB

DR PETE THEXTON · MEMORIAL EXPD. · PAKISTAN 1986 · LOBSANG SPIRE

PROSPECTUS

The prospectus for the expedition was designed by one of the members who was good at drawing. We hoped that our medical research would be more rigorous than his investigations into the national religion of Pakistan, which he seems to have guessed as Buddhism.

In spite of some attempted training through the spring, I was not properly prepared for the expedition. The eight-day walk-in to the Baltoro glacier – the entry point for Broad Peak, the Gasherbrums, and K2, as well as our more modest objective – is the hardest thing I have ever done. We rose each morning before dawn and set out to walk before the sun was hot, but I was not fit or quick enough, and was always the last of the team – nine men and two women – to arrive. There was little drinkable water on the way; the sun was pitiless, the landscape bare and rocky, the air already thinner than I was used to. On one arrival at camp, I drank five pints of green tea in succession before I thought I might sit and wait a little before having another.

The going is rough, the path often uncertain – particularly if you are last and all the porters have disappeared into the distance. The scenery is extraordinary. If you are used to the smaller scale of British mountains, or even Alpine mountains, you get a crick in the neck looking up at the heights of the Karakoram Himalaya, even on the walk-in. For the first few days you are only walking through the junior relations of the massive summits at the head of the glacier, which is surrounded by four of the world's fourteen 8,000 metre peaks. For the first five days of walking – with one rest day in a village – the path is up, down and around the Braldu river, which grinds large boulders in its torrent. When Pete walked this way for the first time in 1978, on his way to a different mountain, one of the team – Pat Fearnehough – fell in the river and drowned while Pete tried to pull him out. It is not a relaxing companion.

Our Base Camp was at Urdukas, which warrants a place-name on the map. In fact, it's just a patch of greenish hillside above the main Baltoro glacier. When we arrived, with our fifty porters, the place seemed like a village. When they had gone, and in between other expeditions passing through to the big mountains – two days' hard walking further east – it felt like the end of the road to nowhere. The glacier below Urdukas is not clean and white, but covered in grey rubble. On the far shore of this dirty frozen sea, to the north, side-valleys led up to massive peaks, framed by ridges of jagged rock running down to vast towers overlooking the Baltoro. Everything was so big, it was hard to get a grip on the scale. We asked our guide how far the other side of the ice was, and he could only answer in time – two hours, maybe (looking at me) three. He had no concept of distance. It was of no use to him.

I spent three weeks hanging out at Urdukas (energetically managing the Base Camp), crossing the glacier, and walking up to the foot of Broad Peak to say goodbye to Pete. One of Pete's old climbing friends, Al Rouse, was the patron of our own expedition. While we were at Urdukas, he was climbing K2 a few miles from Broad Peak. After becoming the first British man to reach the top, he was pinned down in the top camp by a storm. At Broad Peak base camp I recited my poem to Pete, and I said goodbye to Al as well, two men buried high on their last mountains.

I was something of a frustration to the climbers on our expedition, although they were very patient (in my hearing, anyway). I was unwilling to step across a crevasse without being roped up, even if it was too narrow actually to fall down. I wasn't keen on walking across a plank bridge over a 100-foot drop into the Braldu, or wading waist-deep through glacial melt-streams. But I was a sort of mascot as well as Base Camp Manager – perhaps they regarded it as a challenge to get me there and back again.

We were a cheapskate expedition. We had brought very little food with us from the UK, and we bought for ourselves pretty much what the porters eat as daily rations – rice, lentils, flour for chapattis. We were a long way from a shop when we realised how inadequate this was. Our cook was a veteran of many expeditions, and he had never known one like it. He would shake his head and try to make something interesting out of what we gave him. He generally failed. We took a goat (nicknamed "Stew") and a chicken with us, but they didn't go far among 11 westerners and three locals. Living at 14,000 feet is brutally tough. The combination of a low calorie diet, hard walking and the loss of appetite that goes with high altitude stripped the weight off us. I normally weighed about 168 pounds (76kg) at that time – a little more now – but I lost about 35 of those (16kg), even without once getting ill.

When I got home, people said "My God, the hijack must have been an awful experience – look at you!" I had to break it to them that it was the two months before that had made me such a wreck. I don't think you can achieve a result like that in a day. If you could, someone would surely call it a diet and sell a book.

Homeward bound

As this is just a vignette, I'll cut to the chase. The walk out of the mountains was a little quicker than the way in. Fitter, lighter, downhill, and homeward bound, we walked six days without a rest day. We hit Skardu, the last or first town on the edge of the mountains, on September 2, and went in search of decent food. If you have not been on a trip like this, you cannot imagine the obsessive food-fantasies that start to possess people after a relatively short time. We were dreaming of meat, chips, something green, something crunchy…three of the expedition ate too much of whatever was on offer and were sick.

I strolled down the road and bought myself a 7-Up. I had been looking forward to something that wasn't green tea or water mixed with iodine, but I had not anticipated what fizz would do to my contracted stomach. I sat by the side of the road, determined not to throw up in front of the crowd who gathered to watch, probably curious to know where the westerner had managed to get something alcoholic in this dry country. Still, the remainder of the expedition went for a good dinner, and that did for three more. I managed to hold out for the record as Only Expedition Member Never To Have Diarrhoea or Vomiting to the very end.

Our expedition leader shaved his beard off that evening, and we all burst out laughing. He looked about 15 years old without it. The mirrors around the Kashmir Inn showed us that we had no reason to feel superior. I had a straggling beard and a mop of lank hair over my ears, but I thought I would wait for hot water and a sharp razor before I would try to tidy myself up. At least there was a laundry, and we were able to get a few clothes a little cleaner for the journey home.

On the morning of Thursday, September 4, we caught a flight from Skardu to Islamabad, the capital city in the north of Pakistan, and took taxis from the airport to the neighbouring large town of Rawalpindi. On the way in, this had been a 22-hour ride in a bus. Everything seemed easier going home. In Skardu, I had picked up some mail which never made it to Urdukas, and I found that I was expected back at work the following Tuesday. We had booked a very cheap flight with Egyptair which was due to leave Karachi, the large commercial centre in the south of the country, on the Saturday, and would not get home until Tuesday. I never fully worked out why this was, but it seemed to involve a stopover in Cairo that saved a few pounds on the fare and would cost twice as much in hotels and sightseeing. Anyway, I was humming "Homeward Bound" and looking for any excuse, and the idea that I was required for work was enough to get me to the airline offices looking for an earlier flight.

One of the climbers was also keen to get back, and we must have looked an odd couple as we did the rounds of Lufthansa, Swissair, Air France. No luck: they may have had spare seats but simply didn't want us on the plane. Finally, a very helpful local Pan Am clerk spent an hour moving mountains to put me on the next morning's flight from Karachi to Frankfurt. The only available seat was in business class, which priced my friend out of the market. It should, by rights, have been too much for me too. But I had set my eyes on home, and I can't guess what my limit would have been for the ticket.

11

The clerk organised an internal flight that afternoon and hotel accommodation for the night, cleared my credit card, and handed me a bunch of tickets with a broad smile. I feel guilty that I never rang her afterwards to say that I survived; she surely must have wondered, watching the next day's news, what she had got me into.

So I left the others behind that afternoon. Urdukas is in the middle of a big empty wilderness, but base camp is still a close huddle of people living in each other's personal space. It was very strange to be cut loose after so long; also strange to have to take decisions, because the guide and the expedition leaders had usually declared what would happen, where we had to go, when we had to move. Two of my friends came to Islamabad airport to see me onto the internal flight, and after that it was up to me to get myself home.

They were extremely jealous. The cost of my business class ticket was probably the same as the travel budget for the whole of the expedition. We had also heard a rumour that the beer is free in business class. This was a bit like speculation about paradise: one of those things that you can't be sure about because you don't know anyone who's really been there. None of us had had any alcohol for two months. They don't much mind what you smoke in northern Pakistan, but you definitely can't drink. In any event, free booze would probably be a complete waste on me – out of practice and 20% underweight, I would be unconscious after a couple of gulps.

There were a few hurdles still to overcome. Being a mountaineering expedition, and a very low budget one, we had much too much luggage, and quite a lot of it looked interesting on an X-ray machine. We had crampons, ice-axes, pitons, all sorts of metal gear. Best of all were the 'petechiometers'. This is a made-up word for a made-up piece of equipment, so I don't know how it's supposed to be spelt, but it must be something like that. Our medical experiment investigated the fragility of capillaries – small blood vessels – and any correlation between that and the ability to acclimatise to altitude. The theory was that fragile capillaries might have something to do with leaking fluid into the lungs, which is what killed Pete.

Simply being able to say "capillary fragility" at altitude is a reasonable test, but we took it a stage further. The petechiometer applied a standard vacuum to an area of skin with many small blood vessels at the surface – the inside of the bottom lip being the most convenient – for a standard length of time. After a minute, the science team counted the tiny bruises (or petechiae) that resulted from the ruptured capillaries. So we stopped for lip-sucking at all significant stages of the trip – before we left England; in Rawalpindi; in Skardu; throughout the walk-in; at and above base camp. We all kept detailed notes of our pulse-rates on waking up, and our general condition and feeling of acclimatisation. It was considered a good piece of science, and was later published in the British Medical Journal.

The two lip-sucking machines were created by the laboratories at St. Mary's Hospital. Mounted on a metal base-plate about the size of a tabloid newspaper was a small hand-pump for extracting air, connected to a metal bottle from which the air was pumped to create the vacuum, connected to a gauge to measure the pressure, connected to a tube which was put on your lip, with valves to control the flow of air. The plastic tubes weren't wires and the pressure gauge wasn't a clock, but you can't imagine anything that would look more like a bomb unless it really was a bomb. On the way out, three of us had to take one of these through the hand-searches at Cairo airport, and a very stern guard asked us, "Does this explode?" We said, "No", and he waved us on, apparently satisfied.

The day after the hijack, the rest of the team managed to get both of them out through Karachi airport, which remains an astonishing achievement. Perhaps the guards were working on the principle that you couldn't possibly have two bombs on the same plane, or two hijacks in the same airport on successive days.

Anyway, I didn't have a petechiometer in my luggage, but I did have 34kg in a kit-bag and a rucksack, both wrapped up in black plastic and tape to keep the baggage handlers out (although the smell would probably have been equally effective). I know it was 34kg because we weighed them with the spring-balances that were used to share out the loads for the porters. My business class ticket had an allowance of 30kg; we reckoned that I could go 4kg over without being charged. It was very scientific.

The problem was that the internal flight from Islamabad to Karachi had a luggage allowance of only 20kg. I acted (and was) the distressed innocent at check-in, and they let me through. They helpfully ignored the fact that I was wearing two cine-cameras in pouches around my neck, a substantial still camera and a Sony Walkman in a holster on my waist, mountaineering boots, combat trousers, a large red duvet jacket (eccentric in Islamabad at any time of day), and a battered Panama hat. My tatty green carry-on bag weighed 14kg on its own. It was only reasonable, after all – I was well over 14kg underweight in person, so I ought to be allowed the extra luggage to balance up.

Passing through Karachi airport that evening, I met some Australian climbers on their way home. They had climbed Broad Peak as preparation for an attempt on Everest in 1988, Australia's bicentennial year. I had visited them at their base camp, and their doctor talked to me about my brother without knowing who I was. One of their climbers had known him. It touched me to find that other people remembered him there, at the foot of his last mountain. We exchanged greetings and goodbyes.

I have always been paranoid about losing luggage, and also about foreign porters charging ridiculous amounts for moving it five paces, so I struggled to keep sole control of my big bags as far as the free bus to the airport hotel. I was the only passenger. The hotel was a soulless concrete lump not far from the terminal itself – I did not see the sights of Karachi on the way. The booking clerk had told me that the room was included in my fare, and I tried to explain this to the receptionist – well, the person standing behind the desk. I had an impression that he was filling in for a friend on a hot date. He did not seem to understand anything I tried to tell him, but in the end he gave me a key, nodded wisely at my request for an early morning call at three o'clock, and watched me shuffle my burdens up the stairs.

The Karachi airport hotel was not luxurious by British standards, but it had…a soft bed! A bath! Hot water on tap! And…a large, clean mirror, which gave me quite a shock when I stripped off to get in the bath. I was hardly there at all. My spine is normally protected by a layer of something soft, but when I lay down on the hard plastic of the tub, I could feel all my protruding vertebrae crunching against it – I have not had that experience before or since.

At Urdukas, we only had a glacial melt-pool to wash in. That is every bit as cold as it ought to be, and our enthusiasm for washing suffered. After two months of that, a hot bath is a quasi-religious experience. I should have had fresh white clothes to put on afterwards, but I had to make do with an expedition tee-shirt that had seen better days. At least it had been to the laundry within the last week and was not as disgusting as it surely had been on the walk-out. After a wash, I could once again tell which smell was the clothes and which was me.

I reorganised my baggage, packing everything into the green holdall. I established that the television only showed Pakistani programmes. I looked out of the window at a road, a fence, some street lights. I decided that the man downstairs did not know what an early morning call was, so I determined to stay awake all night – having no alarm clock – to make sure that I would catch the plane. So I sat up in the bed, fully dressed – apart from my climbing boots – and dozed, on and off, and on. At 3.15am, I woke with a start, swore at my watch and the receptionist, and gathered up my belongings for what I thought would be the last leg of the journey home.

To the airport

There was no-one in the hotel lobby, so I left the key on the desk and manhandled my bags out to the bus-stop. To my surprise, there was a bus waiting. Again, I was the only passenger – in fact, I had not seen anyone else in the hotel apart from the receptionist. A quiet night in Karachi. Back at the airport, though, there were the usual porters to fend off, and then finally I entered the check-in area.

Here was the first unusual experience of the day. I pay much more attention nowadays to the security arrangements in airports – I am always happy for the inconvenience, as long as the guards appear to be taking their job seriously. But even back then, when I was a little less paranoid, I was surprised to find an X-ray machine set up in the area between the doors and the rows of check-in desks, and a man in a blazer beckoning me towards it. I had never before seen hold baggage X-rayed – it may have been done behind the scenes once checked in, but that was not something I knew or cared about.

The man in the blazer supervised the inspection, then spoke into a walkie-talkie. I was getting the bags back onto a trolley to take to check-in, but he motioned me to wait. "Because we cannot open these bags, I am asking for a sniffer dog to examine them", he explained. I wanted to tell him that this would almost certainly be fatal to any animal with a sensitive nose, but decided that he might not have a sense of humour.

We waited, but no dog arrived. Possibly a succession of them were passing out as soon as they came within 50 paces of my two months' used clothing. I shifted from foot to foot like an incontinent child, keen to be checked in and on my way. After a couple of my mild protests, he shrugged and let me carry on.

Check-in was a relief: I was rid of the big bags. Now I only had my collection of hand-luggage to worry about. After passport control, there was the hand-search and X-ray for that too. They seemed to be taking this extremely seriously. They unpacked – to my considerable dismay – the whole of the green bag onto the search table. It wasn't that there was anything inside that there shouldn't be: it was just that I wasn't sure I could get it all back in again. Quite a lot of it was my film of the expedition – I had borrowed the two cine-cameras from an old climbing friend of Pete's who was a serious film-maker, and had about 90 used super-8 film cartridges to get home. I had also taken reels of still photos with two still cameras, a mixture of colour slides and black-and-white prints. In a digital age, it may be hard to appreciate how much gubbins all this entailed – just as I would probably have no understanding of an early pioneer carrying glass photographic plates.

There were also the cameras themselves and their battery packs. They ran on six chunky "D"-size 1.5-volt batteries mounted on a plastic base-plate with wires to screw into the handle of the camera, and each of the cine-camera pouches had one of these devices in it. After the hijack, one had disappeared. I could not understand what might have happened to it until a few years later I met an FBI agent who told me he had done the "crime scene investigation" on our plane when it returned to Miami. He had some pictures, and asked me to comment on them. There were shots of the exterior and interior of the aircraft, some of the weapons, the damage done in the shootout – and the battery pack of the cine-camera. It appears that it was impounded as being probably part of a bomb, and surely now resides in some FBI vault with the other evidence. Presumably my fingerprints are the most prominent on it. And now immigration officials take my fingerprints when I enter the USA… there is another reason for writing this story now. I am trying to establish an alibi.

At the handsearch, all my items were tagged with a rectangular label on a string. They didn't seem concerned that each passenger was supposed only to have one piece, weighing no more than 5kg (they could hardly have missed that the green bag weighed rather more than that, and they dutifully attached separate tags to the two cine-camera pouches and the still camera holster). There was a further checkpoint at which someone stamped all the tags; and, a little later when we were going out of the building to catch buses to the plane, someone tore all the tags in half. Everything was very methodical, everyone was taking it very seriously. As it turned out, these procedures were also completely useless, but at least the security people were trying.

There was a report afterwards that there had been a very specific warning that there was to be an assault by Palestinian terrorists on an American flag-carrier at Karachi airport during that week. This may have been just a rumour; or they may have received warnings like this every week, and they could not respond to them all. If they really had received a warning, they certainly should have been taking their checks seriously – it was Friday, the attack hadn't happened yet, and this was the Pan Am flight of the day. Of course, they don't pass on such warnings to the passengers, or who would catch a plane?

I entered the departure lounge, and saw a fair crowd of people also waiting for the same flight. Stereotypically, travellers from the sub-continent often have a great deal of hand-luggage – but I think I was winning any competition by weight or number of items that day. It occurred to me that business class passengers should have somewhere special to sit, and after a brief search I found the first class lounge. It wasn't particularly different from the main lounge, apart from being much less crowded, and there were waiters in white jackets bringing round chai – the Pakistani national drink, like tea to the British, but not very similar to our version.

I'm sure that one or two of the looks in my direction carried the thought "there goes the neighbourhood". I put my business class boarding pass in a prominent position on a table to emphasise my right to be there, arranged my luggage around me, put the Panama hat on a chair and accepted a cup of chai (revolting drink, but it was free). Another waiter offered me a choice of magazines, and for half an hour I flicked through *Time*.

We had received no tidings of the outside world since we headed into the mountains. The news in general seemed to be much the same as when I had left, two months before (perhaps the airport only had an old copy – I didn't check). It was the year in which President Reagan ordered the bombing of Libya in retaliation for a terrorist attack on US targets in Germany, and of the Chernobyl nuclear disaster in the Soviet Union; there were articles about glasnost and perestroika. Turning the pages, I came across a piece about Pakistan. The gist was that the military dictator, General Zia ul-Haq, had allowed Benazir Bhutto back into the country during the summer. She was the daughter of the former prime minister who had been executed in 1979 after a military coup; her readmission to the country was the beginning of political liberalisation, the beginning of political opposition – and *Time* was speculating about the likely beginning of political unrest.

I read the article and felt no anxiety. As long as the unrest didn't happen in the airport in the next half hour or so, it wasn't my problem. I didn't plan to be back in the near future.

The terminal building was all on one level. The departure lounge looked out through plate-glass windows onto the runway. The sun had come up and the sky was clear and blue. The airport was not busy at this time of the morning – perhaps 5am – and I cannot remember any other flights landing or taking off. A few other passengers stood by the windows looking for our plane, and there was the minor tension in the air that often inhabits waiting rooms. One white-haired businessman walked past me and commented – he must have assumed that I was a fellow-countryman, on the basis that anyone sitting in a first class departure lounge but looking like a refugee is most likely to be English – "The plane's late, and we only have half an hour in Frankfurt to make the connection for London".

On the plane a little later, I saw him walk past me again, this time with his hands in the air and a gunman behind him, and I muttered, "I don't think we're going to make the connection". This was, I think, my only attempt at a joke during the day, and it was a pretty feeble one. He didn't laugh. There is an adaptation of Kipling's famous line that is probably more true than the original – "If you can keep your head when all about you are losing theirs, you have probably underestimated the seriousness of your situation".

During the expedition, my watch-strap had broken, and my watch was in the holster with the still camera. I looked at it from time to time, but it was not easy to get at through the day, so my idea of the timing of events is not very precise. I believe that the plane finally arrived from Bombay at about a quarter to six, a little late – it was supposed to leave at about six. After a short pause, several big buses brought passengers from the plane to the terminal, and then started to take the economy passengers in the other direction. We were then called to the door; we presented our tagged baggage to a soldier, and filed out to board two small vans. I'm only 5'8", but I had to bend my knees to avoid banging my head as the van buzzed across the short distance to the aircraft. I remember thinking that it was not very luxurious for the posh travellers.

One of the other passengers told me afterwards that he had a premonition at this moment – a voice in his head clearly telling him that something was wrong. Of course, he ignored it – it's not easy to throw away the business class boarding pass your company has bought you and walk back to the terminal building on the strength of a whisper in your head. My feelings were as clear as the sky above. I was looking forward to the sense of relief at having caught the plane.

Pan Am 747
Seat Configuration

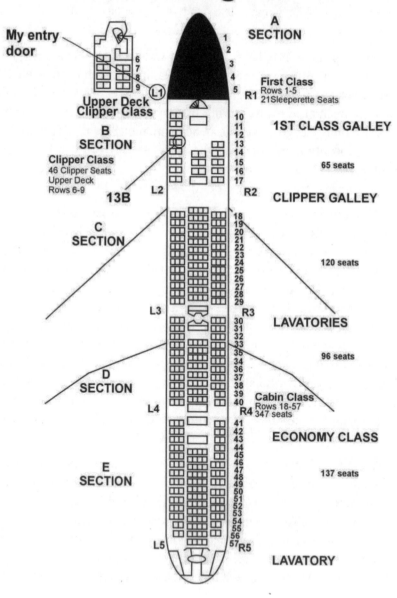

My entry door

A SECTION

First Class
Rows 1-5
21 Sleeperette Seats

Upper Deck Clipper Class

1ST CLASS GALLEY

B SECTION

Clipper Class
46 Clipper Seats
Upper Deck
Rows 6-9

13B

65 seats

CLIPPER GALLEY

C SECTION

120 seats

LAVATORIES

D SECTION

96 seats

Cabin Class
Rows 18-57
347 seats

ECONOMY CLASS

E SECTION

137 seats

LAVATORY

The plane was parked at some distance from the terminal building exit, facing away from the runway. This particular jumbo had five doors on each side – two in front of the wing, one over the wing and two to the rear. Moveable stairways had been run up to the front two doors on the port side. We drove close to the nose, massive above us, and I noticed the name painted on the side – "Clipper Empress of the Seas". A funny name for an aircraft, I thought.

Our vans stopped by the front steps, and we piled out. First and business class were using this staircase, and the rest were going up the second. At the foot of the stairs there were several people – some Pakistani soldiers, with smart uniforms, Lee Enfield 303 rifles, magnificent moustaches and razor-sharp creases in their trousers; another man in a blazer, perhaps a Pan Am official; maybe one or two more. Someone checked the boarding passes, and I climbed the stairs.

An Indian flight attendant in Pan Am uniform greeted me at the doorway. She looked at my pass, and pointed out seat 13B, four rows back on the port side. The first class cabin was forward of the door; business class was in between the two doors. In the centre of the plane, right in front of me as I entered the front door, there was a spiral staircase leading up. I knew that the cockpit would be up there, but I didn't give it much thought. As it happened, on this particular jumbo there were also some additional business class seats in the upper cabin behind the cockpit. There were just eight rows in the downstairs business class cabin – seats considerably bigger than I had ever seen in a plane before, and only six across in three groups of two. Back in economy, the seats were three-four-three (although even that was less crowded than the three-five-three I had enjoyed with Air India the previous year).

The passenger for 13A was yet to arrive, or maybe I was going to have even more room than I had paid for. I heaved the green bag onto my seat, getting ready to put it out of the way for some time. I opened the top of it to get a book out. If I close my eyes and take a deep breath, I can still summon up the feelings in my head in that moment – relief, anticipation, excitement. "I've made it, I've caught the plane. I'm going home. What can possibly go wrong now?" Well...

THIS IS A HIJACK

It begins

I was standing in the aisle with my hands in the bag, looking for "Where the Indus is young" by Dervla Murphy, when I heard a noise from back down the plane. Looking up and back, hands still in the bag, I saw a man struggling with a female flight attendant, just inside the second doorway. She had a telephone in her hand, and he had an arm around her neck. He was dressed in standard Pakistani male clothes – "shalwar-kameez", or a baggy tan cotton shirt and baggy tan cotton trousers – and he had round spectacles and a little moustache. I placed his origin anywhere between the eastern Mediterranean and the Bay of Bengal. In the hand that was on the end of the arm that was around the flight attendant's neck, he had a pistol.

I had what I believe to be a typical civilian reaction to the sight of a gun drawn in anger, which was:

"...............?"

I didn't duck, or go to help, or shout, or run away, or anything. For what seemed like an age, and was probably about two seconds, I gawped. If anything went through my mind at all, it was the thought, "How extraordinary – that man has a gun".

I am told that the SAS rely on this. If they storm a stronghold which contains enemy combatants and civilian hostages, and anyone reacts to them coming in through the windows, they will shoot that person – they can't be a civilian, because the civilians will all freeze. That's quite an important thing to know, but it probably wouldn't matter. I think most people would freeze anyway.

I can't now remember for sure if I actually saw another man, beyond the first, firing a rifle out of the door. I know now that this was happening, and at the time I was certainly aware of gunfire; I had the impression that it was aimed out of the plane. Then there was a noise from the other direction, and I turned again to the doorway through which I had just entered. A man in uniform was standing there, brandishing a rifle and shouting, "Get down, get down!"

My brother, Pete Thexton, at a base camp somewhere in the Himalayas

Pete doing the expedition doctor thing – the backside probably belongs to Al Rouse, who died in Pakistan while I was there in 1986

Photos: unknown climbers – from Thexton family collection

Selecting porters in Skardu for the 1983 expedition

Photo: Greg Child

Pete leading a pitch high on Lobsang
Spire – one sort of mountaineering

On Lobsang Spire – another hippy man

Portaledge bivouac on Lobsang Spire –
looking down the cliff from which the
portaledges are hanging

Photos: Greg Child

Another sort of mountaineering – Pete
(just visible) ascending Broad Peak
near the high camp

The Baltoro Glacier is in the
background, running down towards
Urdukas

Photos: Greg Child

The last descent: Pete returning along the summit ridge of Broad Peak,
K2 in the background

The expedition before the hijack: to Broad Peak Base Camp, 1986

Greg Child was on his way out of the mountains as we were going in – we met in Skardu at the K2 Motel

Urdukas: Base Camp Manager

A local porter carrying a load in the Braldu gorge, 1986

Ghulam the cook thinks about the menu

Chicken dinner for fourteen

The goat, Stew

Standard expedition food

Rachel with one of the lip-sucking machines (see page 12) – try getting that through airport security today

Lip-sucking at high altitude

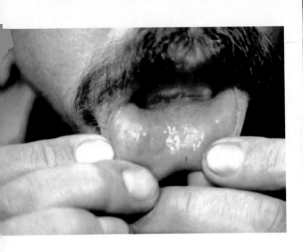

Masherbrum by night

Gasherbrum IV

Lobsang Spire

World's coldest bath

At Urdukas

Back to civilisation, 2
September: eyes bigger than
stomach

Reduced to snorting coke?

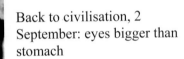

Another reaction that I also believe is typical: I started trying to make sense of what was going on. Imagine a normal departure, when the plane taxis out to the end of the runway and then stops and sits, and sits, and sits. Time passes: the passengers are getting quite restless, wanting to know what's happening. A modern, sensitive pilot might make an announcement to explain. One from the old school wouldn't bother – after all, what is it to do with the passengers? If air traffic control says wait half an hour, then the passengers are going to have to wait along with the plane. But those passengers still want to know what's happening.

Now imagine a somewhat different situation. People are waving guns around, someone is firing, people in uniform are shouting instructions. You might feel even more keen to know what's going on, because now it might just affect what you do, and your life might depend on it. But no-one is going to stop and say, "Oh, by the way, this the Abu Nidal Organisation working to liberate some people from a Cyprus jail". So I made an instant rationalisation of the available evidence. I put together "Benazir Bhutto returns to Pakistan" with "man in Pakistani clothes in second doorway" with "man in uniform in first doorway" with "firing out of the plane" and came up with: "crowd of rioting Bhutto supporters attacking plane; one has made it up the steps; security forces are trying to protect us".

This was impressive reasoning, apart from the fact that I had walked up the steps a few moments before and had not noticed the rioting crowd approaching. At that moment, I was prepared to swear that they must be there, because they were the only thing that made sense of a situation that had gone from very normal to very strange. One subconscious reason for my clutching at this particular straw is probably that it made it "not my problem" – if it was an internal Pakistani dispute, there should be no particular danger for the westerners, beyond the general risk of guns being fired at random. If they were terrorists, that would be a much worse explanation. My mind was not prepared to go down that road until it had to.

This is an important point. In any hijack, the security forces are desperate for information from within the stronghold. Obviously, a released hostage is the best possible source of such information. There is a risk, however, that a released hostage may have built several large castles on the sandy foundation of a little information. The debriefing team will need – very gently, very sensitively – to establish what the hostage has actually seen, and what is interpretation. The interpretation is likely to be rubbish.

Some of this rubbish was going through my mind in the moment that the guard was waving his rifle and shouting "get down". This was a year before the Hungerford massacre burned the shape and name of a Kalashnikov on the consciousness of the British public. In 1986, what the man was holding was just "a rifle", like the guns of the soldiers at the bottom of the steps. He was in uniform, as they had been in uniform. I would not have been able to identify any difference in either the gun or the clothing. However, this was a semi-automatic sub-machine gun which would fire 600 rounds a minute, as opposed to the single-shot rifle. It was not standard issue in the Pakistani military.

Then he turned to the flight attendant who had shown me to seat 13B, and said, "Close the door, close the door!" This was still consistent with my story – protecting the passengers from something happening outside – so that was all right. But when she froze, unable through fear or unwilling through courage to co-operate, he threatened her with the gun. She leaned forward and pulled the door closed, and I struggled to fit this with my comfortable analysis. I also struggled to get down on my seat with 14kg of hand-luggage in the way. There was still no-one in 13A, but it was not easy for me to get to it, so I was perched on top of the green bag – painfully aware that the security guard in the front doorway might take a potshot at the rioting intruder in the second doorway. I was very much in the way.

The next moment was critical to the development of the whole of the rest of the day. One of the other flight attendants had come across from the other side of the plane to try to help her colleague, and had ended up kneeling on the floor close beside the "guard". He called to her to stand up and asked her, "Where is the captain? What is up these stairs?"

The leader of the hijackers had arrived in Pakistan from Thailand – an unsuspicious point of departure – a few weeks earlier, and had been joined by his colleagues who had travelled separately. They had spent some time and effort perfecting their plan. It seems they had checked out the security at the airport and decided that there was no mileage in trying to smuggle guns through the terminal building. So they hit on the simplest alternative: go round the security. They had made up three guards' uniforms– perhaps the budget wouldn't run to a fourth – and acquired a van in which they could masquerade as the police. On the Friday morning, they waited for the plane to land, then tailgated an authorised vehicle through the perimeter gate – possibly with the collusion of the guards, or else relying on their incompetence – and drove across the runway to their target. It wouldn't have been hard to find.

The guards at the bottom of the steps completely failed to stop them running up the stairs and boarding the plane. Perhaps they had taken the precaution of putting rectangular tags on their Kalashnikovs and bags of grenades. In fact, I have great sympathy with people who have to stand guard duty. It is clearly one of the world's most boring jobs, and it is probably often carried out by people who would like to do something more interesting but maybe are not qualified for anything else. The soldiers standing so smartly at the bottom of the stairs had probably been there every day for five years and nothing had ever, ever happened. And then...what you are there for happens so quickly that you fail to react. Ooops! Were we supposed to stop them, do you think?

And yet...and yet...could they have stopped them? There were contradictory stories afterwards, some people saying that the men were carrying forged passes, some saying that they stormed their way through the perimeter (although without apparently inflicting any casualties on people trying to stop them). The guards at the foot of the steps may well have seen a van tearing towards them. When armed, uniformed men jumped out, shouting and running, they may have had the same reaction as me: bewilderment. They may well have challenged them, but they may have had little opportunity to do more than that. They could hardly have shot them out of hand. And, if they had tried harder to stop them, there probably would have been a very unequal fire-fight at the foot of the steps and the same result about ten seconds later – the hijackers on the plane, even more pumped up than they were already.

The bald truth is that, when any hijack is allowed to get this far, everyone involved is trying to sort out a mess that should already have been prevented. From this point onwards, people are likely to die, and the negotiators, the ambulance teams, the firefighters, the commandos are all trying to limit that damage. It should never come to this. If the security around the airport is strong enough, armed hijackers do not get among the passengers. All the effort put into keeping them out of aircraft is a tedious and expensive business for the travelling public, but until there comes a time when we can be confident that there won't be any more hijacks, it's almost as important as making sure that the engines won't fall off.

Anyway, the hijackers had come up with this "brilliant plan", and security people everywhere should remember it. You can put up some very impressive barriers to entry, but it may be possible to go around them. The weakest spot is what they will look for, and here it was pretty weak.

In spite of the ingenuity and care of the rest of their preparation, it is remarkable that they did not know where the pilot sits on a jumbo jet. There is a temptation to expect terrorists and hijackers to be criminal masterminds who plot the attack like a professional commando raid, as they do in films. The truth is that a criminal mastermind probably doesn't get on the plane. The person who leads the attack hasn't been to all the briefings – the mastermind stays safely on shore, knowing that this is a one-way operation. The dupe with the Kalashnikov thinks that he is going to take the plane somewhere and free someone from jail, but what it's really about is publicity for the cause and pain for the enemy. The mastermind probably knows that no-one is going to get out of jail, but that doesn't matter to him.

On a jumbo jet, there are always stairs, and the pilot is always up them. So, a reasonable question might have been, "Where are the stairs?" (although they were fairly obvious to a man standing in the front doorway). But they didn't even know that. I like to think that the leader ran up the steps from the runway, brandishing his gun in front of him, brushing the guards aside, reached the doorway, burst in, turned to the left expecting to see the cockpit, and found – rows of passengers. "Who flies the plane?"

The few seconds this uncertainty created were critical. The flight engineer from our plane later told me what was happening in the cockpit at this time. The flight attendant in the second doorway had shouted some code-words into the intercom telephone. I picture the engineer flicking through the pages of a little book and asking, "Forty-two? Hijack in progress? You don't mean forty-one, passenger taken ill? Or forty-three, passenger in smelly red jacket with too much hand-luggage?" And then he turns to the pilot and co-pilot and says, "She said there's a hijack going on and then she said 'aaargh' and the line went dead. What do we do now?"

What they did on that day, which I hope they would not do today, is decide that the engineer should go and have a look. So he left the cockpit, took the axe out of the emergency equipment store, and went halfway down the stairs. From there, he could see a man in uniform threatening one of his flight attendants with a Kalashnikov, and he decided that he couldn't do much about that with an axe. So he went back upstairs and into the cockpit.

In the upstairs business class cabin, there were seven passengers. Presumably they sat there thinking, "Oh, the engineer's got the axe out. Oh, he's come back up the stairs faster than he went down". And they were still sitting there when the hijackers arrived half a minute later. On that day, I suppose I would have been the same. Today, I think that I would be opening the emergency exit the moment I saw the axe. There are so many lessons that would enable me to deal with it better if it happened to me again (actually, if it happened to me again, I would be very, very annoyed).

The cockpit crew then had a quick discussion about what to do now that they knew there was an armed man downstairs. It seems amazing that this would be something that required discussion. It may be that now there are set procedures to be followed at all times, but in those days, apparently, it was left to the discretion of the pilot in such circumstances, and that meant the pilot was responsible for a difficult judgement call. The engineer said that the vote was 2-1 in favour of immobilising the plane, and that meant leaving.

Let me be very clear about this: on that day, as soon as I realised that they must have gone, I felt enormous relief. I was immediately certain that they had done the right thing. We were surely safer on the ground, stuck fast in a country that I regarded as essentially friendly. Airborne, we would be a menace to other traffic. We could end up anywhere or nowhere. We could even be crashed somewhere to make a big statement. Once the plane was in the air, it would be much harder for the security forces to deal with the situation, and it would be much more frightening for the passengers. I am usually gripping the arm-rests more than is strictly necessary during a routine take-off or landing: the thought that the pilot might have a grenade in his ear would not make it easier.

It was 15 years before a different September hijack made it obvious that you don't ever want the plane to be able to take off. After this hijack, however, the press went for the pilots. I remember a cartoon showing the check-in conversation: *"Smoking or non-smoking? Pilot or no pilot?"* How could the newspapers grab hold such a long way down the wrong end of the stick? And wave it in people's faces so they all believe the same mistaken thing?

There are some good reasons for the pilot to stay. The hijackers will surely deal with the senior person in uniform – "Take me to your leader" – and that would be the pilot. By leaving, the flight crew put the cabin crew in the front line. The pilot is older, more experienced, will have been on more training exercises. Who knows how the relatively inexperienced flight attendants will react?

There are also bad reasons for the pilot to stay – chief among them being the cliché "the captain is last off the ship", and next the thought "these lunatics are not having my plane". Neither of them is nearly as important as the very good reason for going. The pilot can fly the plane: better for everyone if the pilot is not on board.

Another reason the pilot may choose to stay is the thought that escaping will seem like running away. Wherever that pilot is, he may still wonder if he did the right thing, if he could have saved some lives by staying. People may well have whispered behind his back for the rest of his career. No-one can be sure what would have happened – but I am certain he *did* do the right thing, and the whisperers can look at the pictures of the World Trade Centre and hold their tongues.

In the event, the departure of the pilots brought an unpredictable piece of good luck. The cabin crew were probably the best possible people to deal with the situation. In 1985, Pan Am had decided to recruit Indian crews for their flights between India and Europe. This must have seemed an exceptionally glamorous job opportunity, and the people they took on were the best of the best. They all trained together and knew each other, and they had an exceptional "team spirit". Pan Am had a good reputation among its staff in any case – not necessarily among all the flying public, but certainly among its staff – but I believe that the Indian crews were probably better qualified, higher calibre, more dedicated than anyone else in the airline, if not the industry as a whole. Perhaps I am biased, but the events of the day proved me right.

The departure of the flight crew removed three middle-aged, white, American men in uniform, and left instead a group of young, beautiful, Indian women (as well as a couple of men). For example, the senior purser, Neerja Bhanot, was just short of 23 years old, and was a model in between flying for Pan Am. I think that stood a good chance of lowering the temperature and moderating the behaviour of the terrorists.

Of course, these things can work in different ways. Apparently, some of the hijackers were of the more puritanical Islamic persuasion, and were probably immune to the attractions of the female flight attendants. But the leader was definitely very taken with them. As he was in charge, the hostility of the others to the women was suppressed. I believe that there would have been much more temptation to macho posturing and even greater violence if they had been talking all day to an American pilot.

In June 1985, TWA flight 847 from Athens to Rome was hijacked by two Lebanese Shi'ites. The pilot, John Testrake, was forced to fly his plane up and down the Mediterranean from Algiers to the Lebanon, having to land at Beirut airport with six minutes of fuel left after rival militias had fought a battle on the runway. Some of the passengers were dispersed around Beirut, held separately to make a rescue impossible. There is a famous picture of a hijacker and Testrake at the cockpit window, a pistol held in front of the pilot's face. It's surely difficult for a pilot to work out, in the few seconds available, whether the reasons for leaving are "to save my own skin" or "for the safety of the passengers", but there are plenty of reasons under both headings. Many of the passengers (though not all) realised that we were better off on the ground in Pakistan.

The cabin crew simply rose to the occasion, and that could not have been predicted. They were magnificent: calm, professional, showing great bravery in the most difficult circumstances, and doing their best for the passengers throughout.

So, the pilot, co-pilot and flight engineer took advantage of the crucial seconds afforded because the layout of the plane confused the hijackers. They opened an emergency exit in the cockpit roof and slid down a rope to safety. When they hit the ground there was no-one about at all, so they jogged across to the terminal building. The engineer had seen a man in security uniform, and he wasn't sure whether it might be a domestic coup – if they handed themselves in, they might be marched straight back to the plane – but they had no real choice.

In the departure lounge, everything was proceeding as normal. It seems silly, but it's not possible to react instantly to a crisis – there has to be a period when something terrible is happening, and no-one knows. There was a busload of economy class passengers – about 50 of them – who may have been retreating into the terminal away from the gunfire, or they may have been still trying to negotiate their way onto the plane. I can imagine them waving their boarding passes and protesting that *this is not too much hand-luggage, you should have seen the man in the red jacket who was here earlier…* and the guard trying to explain, and eventually getting fed up with them and sending them out to join the rest.

The flight crew presented themselves to someone in uniform in the terminal building and said something along the lines of "We think someone's hijacked our plane, what do we do?" They were taken to the control tower, where the beginning of a response was taking shape.

Back on the plane

Meanwhile, back on the plane… I will refer to the uniformed leader who threatened the flight attendant as 'Abbas', which is what I heard the other hijackers calling him on that day. The flight attendants remember him as Mustafa. Perhaps they used a variety of names to try to confuse the passengers. Neither was his real name.

Abbas sent a second gunman upstairs with Sunshine, the flight attendant whom he had asked about the pilot. In the upstairs lounge they found another cabin crew member and a few passengers. The cockpit door was shut, and the gunman still didn't seem to have a clue. He too asked Sunshine where the captain was, and she indicated the door. He told her to open it, and she said she had no key (although she did). She then stood between him and the door, making sure she was in his way, and shouted for the captain to open up if he was inside – something along the lines of "Captain, there's a hijacker out here who wants to speak to you". After a minute or so the gunman lost patience, pulled her out of the way, and kicked the door open.

The escape hatch is in the roof of the cockpit. The hijacker *still* didn't quite get it. He looked inside, saw no people, and went back downstairs with Sunshine to report to Abbas that there was no-one in the cockpit. Abbas took Sunshine upstairs again to confirm this himself. They searched the cockpit thoroughly. Sunshine had immediately noticed the open hatch, but she tried not even to glance up at it as she helped Abbas to make sure that the flight crew were not hiding under a seat or in a locker. It was only on leaving the cockpit, frustrated and presumably baffled, that Abbas finally looked up. He told Sunshine to close the hatch, and they came back downstairs.

At some point during all this toing and froing, someone shouted, "This is a hijack, put your hands up". I did so, realising that this was more likely to be "my problem" than I had at first hoped. This was one of the worst moments of the day: you read about "a sinking feeling", and I definitely felt it. I'm not sure what it is that is sinking, but it seemed that everything inside me went down a few inches.

After a few moments, Abbas must have taken a decision to deal with the new situation he found himself in – no pilot – and shouted, "Everyone back". They cleared the first and business class cabins to give themselves a secure space from which to control the plane. Like a good civilian, I stood up with both hands in the air; then I thought about my green bag, which I was unwilling to be parted with, so I picked it up and tried to hold it above my head as I walked back. The emergency instructions tell you to leave everything behind when the plane is about to crash – I wonder how many other people would be hanging onto their possessions. "You can't take it with you", they say, but I will probably be trying.

So, I followed a line of people down the port aisle – 15 minutes into my first business class flight, downgraded. The humiliation. In the forward economy cabin, there were some empty seats still – waiting for that busload of passengers left in the terminal – and I spotted one on the window side of the aisle, a few rows in front of the galley and toilet block that divided the first cabin from the second.

When they go through the emergency procedures on a plane these days, they always say, "Take a few moments to identify the nearest exit, bearing in mind that the nearest usable exit may be behind you". There must be some legal reason why they have to point out this possibility on every flight. As I walked down the aisle towards the empty seat, I saw that the nearest usable exit would be behind me – there was a door level with the toilet block. If I had thought about it, I would have worked out that this must be the over-wing exit. I had passed door number two on the way back, and that was unlikely to be usable because an armed man took up position at the front of the cabin, standing in the port aisle.

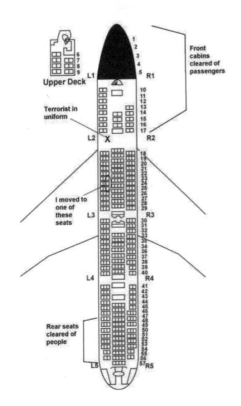

Front cabins cleared of passengers

Upper Deck

Terrorist in uniform

I moved to one of these seats

Rear seats cleared of people

I put the green bag on the floor, where it failed to go under the seat in front, so I sat down with my knees up and my feet on the bag. The seats in economy were definitely a lot smaller and a lot closer together than the one I had just left. I held my hands above my head, and looked cautiously to left and right. On my right, the people from the seats in front of mine came filing past, including the white-haired Englishman (and I made my feeble joke about missing connections). People sat in the aisles, and further back, they sat in the spaces by the doors, toilets and galleys. The rear cabin was half-cleared in the same way, so most of the passengers and crew on board – about 380 people in all – were compressed into two-and-a-half cabins, with a few others left forward by the front door and in the upper cabin. Low-fare airlines might want to take note – you can get a lot of people into a jumbo jet this way.

On my left, a man and a woman were seated, looking as if they had probably come back from the first class seats. They were middle aged (I thought at the time – I would probably now call them a young married couple), and they looked to me to be American, and possibly Jewish. The first thought that passed through my mind was, "They're in front of me". That's a brutal thing to think, but I believe that I was not the only person looking for this small crumb of comfort. On the floor beside me, a Pakistani man had his arm around his teenaged daughter and was whispering to her, "It will be all right, insh' Allah" (God willing). I was thinking, "Yes, God willing, it will be all right".

But the man was probably looking up at the westerner in the aisle seat and thinking, "He's in front of us". Everyone was looking for someone worse off than them. The married couple looked grey with fear – they probably couldn't see anyone. "I'm in front" is not a good thought at this point.

There were some announcements on the public address system in a foreign language. They remain burned into my memory: "Habbady-aah! Hayayabbady-aah! Habbaddy-abbady-aaah!" I can remember these words precisely and accurately because I was sitting there trying to work out what they meant. I didn't even know what language it was, but I was so desperate to know what was going on, I was willing to make a very uneducated guess from the sound alone. It could have been a list of demands, or some prayers, or a weather forecast, but it sounded to me like a set of orders – "John, go to the back of the plane! Bill, guard the doors! Bert, where's the ammunition?" On that basis, I decided that there were a lot of them, because it seemed like a long list.

That was my main reason for thinking that there was someone specifically watching me, someone standing behind me with a gun; but I think that many of the passengers formed the same opinion. The word "terrorism" is so overused – so much a "global political problem" – that people may forget what it means to be *terrorised*, individually and personally. They had not done anything particularly violent to anyone – not yet – but they had definitely deprived me of the power of rational thought. My brain would not work properly. For much of the day, they had two men watching about 380 passengers in those two-and-a-half cabins – most of the people could not even be seen by any of their captors. But I am quite sure that most of us were completely under control, certainly at this point and probably for a long time afterwards. No-one was going to try to do anything, for instance to try to escape, because of the man behind them with the gun.

At this stage of the day, the hijackers could have left the plane, gone to the terminal building, had a hearty breakfast, bought some duty-frees and come back, and we would still all have been sitting there with our hands in the air. I don't know how long it would have been before someone would have said, "I think they've gone, we can leave" – I think it would have been a long time. Later on, if a masked commando had opened a door and said, "Come on, get out now", I think many passengers would have refused to move – "Shut up! Go away!" would be the natural reaction. I have heard that the SAS had to carry people bodily out of the Iranian Embassy at the end of the famous siege – that may have been because the building was on fire and they were in a hurry, or it may be that some people were too frightened to move.

This small-scale terror can be very effective. The mere threat of violence is often enough to control a large number of people. If ever your captives look as if they might recover their initiative, you can threaten them again. If that doesn't work, shoot one – that should make the point very well.

And yet – the whole psychology of the situation changed halfway through September 11, 2001. What happened to United flight 93 is not absolutely clear, but it seems certain that people realised that they were going to die anyway, so they might as well fight; they did so, heroically, but failed to take control back and save their lives. Now, there might be a few thinking along those lines even at this point, with the plane still on the ground and the doors only just closed. That would not necessarily be helpful; it would certainly be different.

I tried to get a grip on myself. I told myself, "People get off hijacks". Surely someone would die, but there was no reason it should be me. After all, it seemed likely that the Americans would be first, and there were surely a good many Americans on a Pan Am flight. I resolved to do what I was told, and to try to make myself inconspicuous. I realised that wearing a red duvet jacket was not the best start in that direction, but I used my raised hands to brush the Panama hat off my head and into my lap. I sank down a little in the seat, so that only my hands would be visible. Now, I could lean very slowly to my right and look up the aisle to see a uniformed man with a handgun – not Abbas – standing in the doorway between economy class and the business cabin. If I moved very slowly, I did not think that the gunman behind me would object. In fact, the nearest gunman behind me was two cabins away.

The next announcement was in English, spoken by a female. One or other of the flight attendants made all the remaining announcements through the day. The first was surreal: "Ladies and gentlemen, the group responsible apologise for the inconvenience caused. Their argument is not with you, they do not wish to hurt anybody; but if you make any sudden movements, you will be shot". The cabin crew had a variety of messages to relay. Sometimes they were chilling warnings like that; sometimes they were about coffee or sandwiches. Each one always started with "Ladies and gentlemen", as if everything was completely normal. They never let a tremor into their voices. On the other hand, they never tried to give us any encouragement of their own, as a pilot might have done – "I'm negotiating with these guys, and it's all going to be OK". They just told us what they had to tell us, very professionally.

I think that was exactly right, and it helped everyone stay calm. The warning was scary, but you could think, "OK, I won't make any sudden movements, I won't get shot". If they had tried to give us hope, then that hope could have been disappointed – probably better to keep everyone in a very even state of mind.

The next announcement asked those sitting by the windows to pull the blinds down. The gunman from the front of the cabin walked down the aisle and waved his gun at one or two people who had not fully closed them. Now, we were sealed off: we could not see out, and the people outside could not see in. It was very quiet: there was no panic, no protest, no children crying. There was the hiss of the air conditioning in the background, and the plinky-plonky music that they play before an international flight takes off. This was on an endless loop – it went round and round, all day. There may have been more than two songs, but the ones etched into my memory are "The Entertainer" and "New York, New York". Good tunes, but a little tiresome on the fiftieth rendition in a row. Flight crew, you should definitely escape: but think about taking the tape with you as you go.

The people who sell background muzak claim that there is a reason for playing it: to allow people to have quiet conversations without being overheard. It probably was useful for that purpose on the day. It was possible to whisper without feeling conspicuous, although conversation was limited. I asked the man next to me, "Where are you from?" He replied, "North America". He didn't want to be more specific. Perhaps he thought he could pass for Canadian. They probably wouldn't hate Canadians.

So the blinds were down, the muzak played, and we were left to our thoughts. I was beginning to realise that the pilots must have escaped, or been killed, because there was no word from them, and the engines were not starting. Surely we would be hearing from the pilot if he was there; surely we would be flying somewhere. I started to feel a great deal better about the situation. "This will be all right", I told myself.

We sat with our hands in the air for – I don't know how long. My watch remained in the holster on my waist throughout the day. Perhaps half an hour, perhaps an hour, perhaps an hour and a half. Try it. Afterwards, journalists asked me, "Did they beat you?", and I could sense their disappointment when I said that they did not. Holding your hands in the air isn't very interesting, it won't sell newspapers. But it's important to appreciate that a relatively minor discomfort, spread over a long period and combined with absolute terror, is about as intolerable as being physically beaten.

In a way, I think it would be better for some people if they were beaten – that would make them, as well as everyone else, realise how tough it was. After sitting in the same seat for a day, two days, a week, you will be pretty disgusting when you come out. You will be an object of shame and horror. There is a temptation to think that you have failed, that you have let yourself down – but it is not so. They did this to you; they put you in a situation that could not be borne. Whatever your state, you have to hold your head up and know that you did your best.

After the hijack, I met a number of people who had been through similar experiences – usually, I felt that I had got off lightly. I met Mrs Sheila Matthews, who was held hostage in her flat in Balcombe Street, London by an IRA gang in 1975. They made her sit in the same chair for six days, and did not allow her to leave it for anything. For anything! How can you do that to a 53-year old woman who has done nothing at all to you? The effect of that level of cruelty is easy to underestimate. Other people – including journalists – may not understand it without visible scars and gory details, and it will be hard enough for the victim to see it that way. It's an important part of getting over it.

After a while, the female voice told us over the PA that we could lower our hands onto our heads, but we must make no sudden movements; then, we could lower our hands into our laps, as long as we did it slowly. This was a great relief, not only for the aching muscles and the circulation, but also for the invisibility it allowed. I was now huddled down in my seat, knees up, hands in my lap, hat somewhere on the floor. I could not be seen at all by the man at the front, and the man behind me hadn't done anything alarming yet. If I leaned sideways, very slowly, I could get a glimpse of the terrorist with the gun, but he didn't seem to be taking any particular interest in me. I seemed to have achieved objective number one: remain inconspicuous.

The next announcements were even more encouraging: "If anyone on board has a transistor radio, could they please put their hand up" – someone must have done so, because I saw them listening to one later – and then, "If anyone on board knows how to operate the cockpit radio, could they please identify themselves". This was very good news. First, it showed that they were not very good at hijacking – they did not have all the equipment they needed, and they did not have the expertise to operate the radio themselves. Second, it showed that something had gone very wrong with their plans, and they needed help from the passengers.

Most importantly, it confirmed my growing suspicion that the pilot was not there – the pilot would surely be able to work the radio. So we were not going anywhere. I had no particular idea about where this group was from, but I could think of several places that I did not want Islamic terrorists to take me. There were already hostages in Beirut – John McCarthy had been taken in April 1986, and he was not freed until August 1991. It was unlikely that any journey would take us to a better place than Pakistan.

I began to feel really quite safe. I was curled up almost in a foetal position, crammed into a confined space, studying the back of the seat a few inches from my face – it was quite easy to turn off the world and pretend that this was not really happening, not really threatening. The music and the drawn-out quiet, the calm atmosphere in the cabin, added to the sense that this was only a mildly disturbing dream, somewhat removed from reality.

Perhaps this is why I completely missed the first death. After maybe two hours – sometime after 8 o'clock – Abbas came down the port aisle and took a man from a seat. Rajesh Kumar was Indian by birth, but had recently obtained American citizenship. He had come back to Bombay to collect his elderly grandmother so that they could go together to the USA to celebrate his new status. So, he happened to be an American – but Abbas could not possibly have guessed that by looking at him. He asked the first few people where they were from, apparently looking for an enemy – but after the first two had said "Pakistan" and "India", he seemed to lose patience and grabbed the next person. He was just "the nearest body".

Kumar was made to kneel behind the front door, and one of the flight attendants stood in the doorway with a megaphone and passed on Abbas' demands for a new crew. The response was that the pilots had hurt themselves jumping down from the cockpit and a different crew would take a while to find. Abbas gave them twenty minutes.

As he was kneeling behind the closed door, knowing what this was likely to mean, as confused as everyone else about what was going on, Kumar said to the flight attendants, "I'm an American citizen". This was definitely the wrong thing to say. He must have thought, like me, that this was a Pakistani revolution – he wanted to say that he was not a local, not involved. Sunshine told him, "Shut up, he's against Americans". She did not think Abbas heard. Telling them who he actually was would probably have confirmed his death sentence, but I think he was just sitting in the wrong place at the wrong moment: he was in an aisle seat, conveniently nearby. They just wanted a body – they didn't particularly need anyone specific. It's that simple, that brutal.

Sitting in my safe haven a few rows back, I was completely unaware of Kumar being taken. I did not hear his protests, I did not see him go forward at gunpoint. I was too busy making myself inconspicuous and feeling secure, also sitting invitingly in an aisle seat, just as he had been.

Abbas negotiated for some time – maybe thirty minutes, maybe an hour – with his bargaining counter kneeling behind the front doorway. The demand for an aircrew to take the plane was very unlikely to be met. Kumar begged for his life and Abbas taunted him – asked him, "Are you a man? Then why are you crying?"

After the expiry of the deadline, the negotiators outside the plane arrived with a telephone that they proposed to get on board to help communications. Abbas seemed to lose his temper. He stood Kumar in the doorway, shot him in the back and threw him out of the plane, tossing the gun out after him. His body lay for a while under the plane while the negotiators tried to establish that it would be safe to send people in to carry him away.

The passport raffle

After perhaps three hours on the plane – maybe at about nine o'clock – the female voice made a further announcement. "Ladies and gentlemen, please hold your passports above your head, and they will be collected". I suppose that we all knew this was likely to happen, but I had not given much thought to what I would do when the order came. I was trying not to think about anything at all.

It would clearly be best not to hand the passport in. Once you have done so, you are identifiable by name, photograph, nationality. If you have not done so, you are an anonymous member of a crowd. If you have not done so and other people have, you are almost certainly now at the back of the queue.

A few years later, I was contacted by a representative from a company who wanted my views on their plan to make false passports – documents which appeared to identify the bearer as belonging to some wholly inoffensive country. The idea was that you would carry one of these to hand in, instead of your own, if you were ever hijacked – so you would not be picked out as American, or British, or Israeli, or whoever it was that you thought the hijackers were after. I suppose you never know what people will buy – maybe the sales of tin hats when Spacelab was coming down were apocryphal, but this plan was of the same order. The likelihood of getting hijacked is tiny (as I say to my wife, "Don't worry, who do you know that has ever been…oh"). The possibility that one of the company's customers would be among the hijacked few is at the vanishing point. Then, of course, they would have forgotten to bring the false passport with them on that trip; or they would have been hijacked by the one group in the world that really hates citizens of Utopia.

It's also likely to be illegal to try to make things that look like passports but aren't. I gave my frank views, and have never seen them on sale. Perhaps I saved someone from a commercial disaster, if not an airborne one.

I was so under the hijackers' control, so full of "Do what you are told", that I took my passport out of the camera holster where I was carrying it. My main thought was, "If they search us later and find I haven't handed it in, I'll be in real trouble". A couple of brain cells functioning properly would tell me that you cannot search 380 people crammed into half of a jumbo jet. You are unlikely to be able to tally off the people who have handed in their passports – you will be hard-pressed even to make a reliable count of the people, when they are tucked around in the doorways, crowded on the floor, squashed in the galleys. "We've got 358 people and 325 passports – no, was it the other way around?"

None of that occurred to me as I held the rectangle of blue-black cardboard with its gold crest up. In the days before the standardisation of European Union passports, a British one looked quite different from most of the others. There are those who regretted its passing as a final goodbye to Empire and all that, but they have probably never had to hand one in during a hijack.

One of the flight attendants was coming down the cabin with a holdall, collecting the passports as they were handed to her. Then there was a further announcement: "Ladies and gentlemen, if your passport is in the overhead lockers, do not get out of your seats". The implication was that they could stay there, that you did not have to hand a passport in. The couple beside me both sighed with relief. Their passports may have been forward in their hand luggage or they may have been in their pockets, but wherever they were, there they would remain.

I was sitting like an idiot with the passport waving at the end of my outstretched arm. I thought about quietly lowering my hand, or doing a magic trick and dropping the thing back down the sleeve of my duvet jacket. But I thought the man standing behind me (in fact, two cabins away) would have seen this, so I thought it was safer to let the attendant take it. I have made better decisions.

In fact, the Pakistani man in the aisle took it out of my hand and passed it forward. Perhaps he was thinking, "British passport, get that in the bag – he's in front of us".

The flight attendant passed by and went to the rear cabins. The voice made a further announcement: "Sunshine, come back with what you have got". She went forward again, and I was left with a more uncomfortable feeling.

What I did not know was that Sunshine was doing something extremely brave, selfless and clever. She knew that Abbas was looking for Americans, so she determined not to give him any. However, she did not think that it would be credible for there to be no Americans at all on a Pan Am flight. So she put American passports with Indian or Pakistani faces into the bag, but concealed all the white faces. Some she discarded, dropping them under seats, putting them in pockets or behind cushions. At some points, she thought the hijackers were watching her too closely, so she had to hide them in her own clothing.

One white American man noticed what she was doing and said, "Oh, Miss, you've dropped my passport". Perhaps, in the interests of improving the human gene pool, she should have put it in the bag. But he was probably like me: desperate to do what he was told.

How they would have reacted if they had found the passports, had realised what she had done – well, it was an act of extreme courage. The most remarkable thing about it, to my mind, is that she didn't have to do anything other than obey orders – it was, in effect, "not her problem". No-one would have dreamed of criticising her for simply doing what she was being told to do at gunpoint. Hardly anyone would have thought of what she decided to do. Her bravery, quick thinking and ingenuity astonish me still, after all these years.

When she returned to the front of the plane, she tipped out the passports in a big pile, and Abbas told her to sort out the Americans from the rest. One of the others helped. Sunshine opened each one as the other woman passed it to her, and found three more white faces whose passports must have been handed to her in bundles by helpful passengers. She hid them at first under her legs, then tried to force them under a seat cushion, having to make distracting noises by shuffling the passports with her feet when she discovered the cushion was held down by Velcro.

So she finally handed over the edited pile of American passports. Abbas picked them up, one by one, and was told, "No, look, an Indian face". So he next looked at the British ones. There were probably about twenty British nationals on the plane, of whom maybe only half a dozen were Anglo-Saxon in name and appearance.

The next announcement was: "Ladies and gentlemen, would Mr Michael John please identify himself".

Those are my first two names, and I knew it had to be me. I wasn't going to put my hand up and ask, "Do you mean me?", but I was sure they would add my surname in a minute. So I sat, staring at the back of the seat ahead of me, wondering why, and feeling a churning in my guts and in my head, and knowing that they were going to shoot me.

Perhaps they've seen my tee-shirt, which says something about St. Mary's Hospital, and they want a doctor. That might be difficult, because I am not a doctor, but I was willing to give it a go... no, they want to shoot me.

Perhaps my parents have got a message through about my brother dying, they're going to let me off the plane on compassionate grounds. No, my parents don't even know I'm on the plane (as well as the small likelihood of any compassion). They want to shoot me.

I could not understand it, could not believe it. Where were the Americans when you needed one? How were the British first, how was I first?

A few minutes passed, or maybe a few seconds, or maybe a lifetime, while I tried to keep a grip on myself. Then: "Ladies and gentlemen, will Mr Michael John Thexton please come to the front of the plane."

I thought for a moment about staying where I was. I knew that my passport photo was clean-shaven and short-haired, and I didn't look like it at all. Could I sit it out, denying that it was me? The problem with this plan was my paranoia about losing luggage. While waiting in the departure lounge, I had written my name on all the tags – two for the cine-cameras around my neck, one for the holster on my waist, one on the big green lump I had dutifully carried back and put under my feet. If they were looking for Thexton, and no Thexton came forward, it was unlikely that they would give up. When they started to search the cabin, the tags would be a bit like a balloon over my head. "Here's Mike!"

Until 2003, in 30 years of flying I had never lost my luggage, but I had been hijacked. Now that I have been through both these experiences, I can say with authority that losing your luggage really doesn't measure up as a scary experience. It still bothers me, though.

So I realised that I had to go forward. I was sure that they were going to shoot me, and I felt sick and weak, but I stood up. I said what might have been my last words – "For f***'s sake!" – and picked my way between the people sitting in the aisle. I've often wondered about my mother asking, "Did he have some last message for us?" Well, that would have been it.

Sitting near me was an American-resident Indian family. Their three year old daughter saw the bedraggled, long-haired, wild-eyed man get up and go forward, and for some time afterwards, she would ask her parents, "What happened to the hippy man?" They had no way of knowing that I had survived. It was not until 2004 that they were able to tell their daughter what became of me.

I put my hands above my head again and approached the man standing at the front of the economy cabin. He watched me without apparent interest. "That's me, they've called me forward", I said to him. He nodded, and waved his gun to indicate that I should go past. I stepped once again into the business class cabin, and looked ahead. The seats were all empty, apart from the two pairs immediately aft of the front door, where four female flight attendants were seated. Abbas was standing in the aisle beside them, a pile of passports at his feet, one in his hand.

I have a strange memory of another man, possibly a Pakistani, passing me in the aisle, going aft with his hands in the air and a relieved expression on his face. I doubted if anyone Pakistani could really have misheard the name "Thexton" and thought it might be them, so I had no idea what he might have been doing there. This man had asked to go to the lavatory shortly after Kumar had been shot, and Abbas invited him to come to kneel in the doorway instead. He had spent some time praying in the Muslim fashion, and now had an answer to his prayers. He was even allowed to go to the lavatory.

As I walked slowly forward, I was able to get a good look at Abbas. He had taken his shirt off and was showing off his form – athletic, muscular, over six feet tall. He looked very much a soldier, very much in control of himself and the situation (even if it wasn't going his way). I've already mentioned the temptation to exaggerate the professionalism of hijackers – they may well not plan their operations with as much skill and forethought as commandos – but it is also possible to exaggerate their negative qualities. After September 11, I read many descriptions referring to "madmen". The word conjures up in my mind a much poorer specimen than Abbas, physically and emotionally. It would be a mistake to believe that he was mad. On that day, he was – if you can detach yourself for a moment from the evil he was engaged in – impressive. If you put him in a line-up with 20 other people, and invited people to "pick a leader", most would have had no difficulty in choosing Abbas.

I studied the rifle quite closely. I did not recognise its make, but then I knew nothing about guns. What I did notice was that there was brown sticky tape around the magazine, and it hung around his shoulders on what appeared to be a crepe bandage rather than a proper leather strap. My mind was rapidly emptying itself of all rational thought, and I can remember thinking, "Bandages and sticky tape? Bandages and sticky tape?" Later I saw – as some will immediately have guessed – that the sticky tape was to hold together two magazines. The Kalashnikov would empty a magazine very quickly, and he had another one right there when he needed it.

I also noticed that there was a whitish band sticking out above the waistband of his trousers. I guessed at the time that this was something like a boxer's protection, in case someone tried to kick him in the balls. I was told afterwards that it was a strip of plastic explosive that he carried around his waist, and tried to detonate at the end (by getting one of his colleagues to shoot at him – not the most effective method).

Some journalists afterwards asked me, "Did you think of jumping him?" Well, he was a good-looking boy, but there's a time and a place for these things... ah, I suppose they thought I might try to overpower him. They had obviously watched too many films, and not paid attention to what I looked like. Here was I, 130 pounds, five-feet-eight, unarmed and terrified, facing up to a six-foot-plus musclebound soldier with an automatic rifle and who knows what else, probably trained to kill me with his bare hands as soon as look at me. No, I did not think of jumping him.

The strange thing is that today I *would* be thinking of it. September 11 changed everything. Before that, in a plane-load of passengers there might be one or two who would be thinking of it, and in ten hijacks you might get someone who would actually try something. On United flight 93, the passengers – standing for all the passengers on all the flights over all the world – realised that they would probably die anyway, so they might as well have a go. One of the passengers talked to the emergency operator on his mobile phone, said a short prayer, and led some of the others forward with the famous words, "Let's roll". No-one knows for sure what happened then, but it seems likely that the struggle for control of the aircraft led to its crashing in Somerset County, Pennsylvania, rather than on the likely target, the Capitol building in Washington.

Today, even I would be looking for an opportunity, walking down the aisle with my hands in the air, to do something heroic, suicidal and futile.

While the plane is on the ground, it's probably not helpful. As long as the plane has not taken off, the negotiators would almost certainly prefer to keep everything calm and peaceful. The likelihood that many passengers would now be at least minded to try, increasing the statistical likelihood that someone actually would do so, may not be a good thing at all. Once the plane is in the air, of course, everything is different. The negotiators probably would still want to try to talk it down, but they might not be given the chance.

Anyway, on that day, I was certainly a light year away from jumping him. I walked up, wondering what to do, whether there was anything I could do. He looked at me, and looked down at the passport, open in his hand.

"You are Michael John Thexton?"

"Yes." (Perhaps I should have tried, "Oh! Sorry, I thought you said Sexton...")

"Where are you from?"

I actually thought for a split second of saying, "I'm from Belfast, and long live the revolution, and down with these imperialist filth...". But I didn't think he would recognise my attempt at a Belfast accent, or know the difference, or believe me. Besides, it said where I was from in the passport. He was really checking up that the right person had come forward. "I'm from London."

He pointed to the camera pouches hanging across my chest. "What are these?"

"They're cameras, I've been making a film."

He beckoned to one of the flight attendants. She unhooked the straps from my shoulders, unzipped the cases and showed him.

"They're cameras." They were put aside, and he pointed at the holster. She opened that, and showed him the tape recorder and still camera. They disappeared as well.

"Are you a soldier?"

I was taken aback by this question. I suppose my passport photo looked sufficiently clean-cut – maybe they had picked mine as the most likely to make trouble for them, possibly the youngest British Anglo-Saxon man aboard, the highest-ranking "enemy". I was taken aback, but my answer was immediate: "No, I'm a teacher, not a soldier".

I was telling a friend this story a week later and he interrupted me – "You really can't bear to admit you're a chartered accountant, can you?" Well, I thought that "chartered accountant" sounded too "capitalist imperialist", and "teacher" was a good street-credible profession the world over (except perhaps in some periods of anti-intellectual revolution – that would be just my luck). I teach accountants, so it was fairly true, if not quite "true and fair" (that's how an accountant would look at it, anyway).

Lastly, he looked me in the eye – I was half-avoiding his gaze, trying not to look challenging, but having to look back at him when spoken to – and asked, "Do you have a gun?"

I burst out laughing. I was close to hysterics of the uncontrollable kind, I suppose. I spread my hands out, and shrugged my shoulders. "I haven't got a gun. You've got all the guns around here." I've always wished that I had told him I was clean, I'd been through the security checks – but perhaps, as I was saying, there is a time and a place.

"Kneel here." He pointed to the space behind the door. I tried to tell him that my brother had died in the mountains, that my parents had no-one else, please don't hurt me... but he waved one hand as if to say, "I'm too busy for all that", and put the other hand on my shoulder. It did not take much pressure to make my knees bend.

I have studied these doors quite closely. They appear to open by tilting – the rear edge coming in (or perhaps staying still), the forward edge going out – then they swing out to the side. This door was "cracked open", with a strip of daylight showing at the rear edge, but the bulk of the door still blocking the opening. The windows in the doors do not have blinds, so it's always possible to see out in case of an emergency – my eyes were level with the window, and in its narrow frame I could see the sun shining on the concrete runway, a fire engine and a soldier in the distance. They were part of a different world.

The flight attendants were crying. I knew what was happening, but they had seen it all half an hour before – they *really* knew what was happening. I thought I would be the first. On a gruesome level of detail, there was nothing in that doorway to show what had already happened to Rajesh Kumar. I suppose that Abbas had opened the door to shoot him, or cleaned up thoroughly afterwards, but there was no sign of their earlier murder.

Abbas stepped forward quickly and glanced out of the window, then paced up the aisle a few rows, reached across, lifted a blind and glanced out again. Then he walked back and spoke to one of the flight attendants.

"Tell him that if anyone comes near the plane, if any US troops come near the plane, we will kill one body immediately. And tell him I have bombers on board, and all my men are commandos."

His English was quite good. "One body" was probably a reasonable expression of how he regarded me – how he regarded all of us. We were trading stock: we could be bargained over, or disposed of.

The flight attendant relayed this message to someone I could not see, who was standing beneath the nose of the plane. This was Viraf Daroga, who had taken charge of the negotiations at the beginning. He is a Pakistani national, and was at the time the local Pam Am station chief. It may seem strange that there was no trained police or army negotiator out on the front line at this point, several hours into the hijack, but the science of negotiation had not spread that far at that time. There are good and bad places to be taken hostage – sadly, the places with the worse negotiators are probably the places it is more likely to happen. "Take this plane to London Stansted" is a good thing to hear your hijacker say. I believe that the Pakistanis have undertaken training since, but like all good door-closing exercises, I don't think that they have had a horse bolting after 1986. Not a hijack of a jumbo jet, anyway.

The man from the airline was, even so, doing his very best. His response was, "Tell him that there is a member of the Pan Am ground crew on board who can operate the cockpit radio. If he talks to us on the cockpit radio, we will withdraw everyone from around the plane. Tell him that there is no need to hurt anyone."

Abbas didn't seem to quite catch that, so the flight attendant relayed the message. Kneeling in front of him, I couldn't see his expression, but he sounded surprised and puzzled. "But we have asked for someone to operate the cockpit radio. Why has this man not identified himself already?"

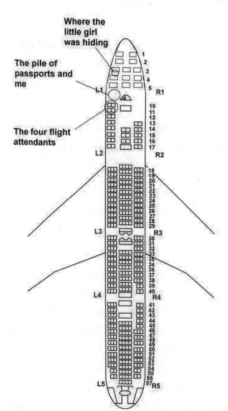

Where the little girl was hiding

The pile of passports and me

The four flight attendants

From my position on the floor, I could think of several good reasons.

So an announcement was made, specifically asking for the Pan Am ground crew member on board. I was told later that three men stood up, which may or may not be true, but one of them walked up the port aisle, a Pakistani with a workman's toolbelt around his waist – screwdrivers, pliers and so on tucked into loops and clips. Abbas stepped forward to meet him, holding the rifle in one hand, undoing the belt with the other, tossing it into one of the luggage bins, patting him down, directing him to go upstairs.

The station chief knew from the beginning that he had someone aboard who could operate the radio, but quite understandably he did not want to identify his own employees. Until Rajesh Kumar was shot, he could not be sure that Abbas would carry out his threats. Once Kumar was dead, he knew that there would be killings in succession unless they got something. So he had to give them Meherjee Kharas, who spent the day working the radio for their negotiations, and who died in the shooting at the end. One of the reasons you want a trained negotiator is that they have been taught to understand that this is not their fault; they do their best to sort out the mess, but the mess is of the terrorists' making, and if people die, it is one hundred percent the terrorists' fault, nothing to do with the negotiators. They get proper debriefing and counselling afterwards to reinforce that truth. The station chief probably still believes, wrongly, that the death of Kharas was somehow his fault.

On the other hand, it is half-true that he traded Kharas for me. I was off the immediate hook because the other man had gone upstairs to work the radio. Even so, at this point and for most of the rest of the day, I would have put the odds strongly on Kharas to live and on me to die. I was lucky and he was not. The police negotiator is also able to walk away at the end of the operation: the airline boss had to visit his employee's widow. I can only imagine how he felt and how he feels, and be grateful for what seemed at the time to be a very effective piece of bargaining.

At this moment, it is inconceivable that I will survive the day. I picture it like the end of an old episode of Batman: our hero is on the conveyor belt edging towards the circular saw, chained and unconscious, with the Riddler's goons standing around laughing, and the voice asks, "Can Batman get out of this one?" Well, yes, of course he can. But can Mike Thexton get out of *this* one? Not a chance. There had to be a demand at some point that would not be met, and then they would shoot me. People get off hijacks, but people get shot; I had gone from "it doesn't have to be me" to "it's obviously going to be me".

Saying prayers

Another man came down the stairs and stood guard over me, still kneeling in the space behind the door, beside the pile of passports. The door was shut. I was no longer in a position to see anything but sky out of the window. The four flight attendants still sat in the four seats aft of the doorway. I felt sick to the bottom of my soul.

Strangely, perhaps, the main thing I felt was sadness for my parents, not for myself. I think that this was probably helpful throughout the day, and afterwards. I had spent three years thinking about going to the foot of Broad Peak – first as a daydream, and more recently as a plan, then as an arduous and epic journey. I had just fulfilled my most urgent ambition. I would prefer to come back and get on with my life, but I did not have such a strong feeling of unfinished business as I might have had. Also, I had spent much of the previous two months thinking about death – generally my brother's, but quite often my own (when contemplating river crossings and crevasses). I was mentally prepared.

For my parents, on the other hand, I knew that this would be ghastly. They had been shattered by Peter's death, and here it was going to happen again. I knew that they had felt all the irrational fears a parent can feel when they said goodbye to me – they took me to Heathrow Airport, just as they had taken Peter three years before, and seen me disappear behind the security screens, and they had never said a word, never suggested that I should stay, that it might be too dangerous. I am sure that they must have felt it. There is a famous poem about watching your child walk away: it ends, "love is proved in the letting go". My parents chose it for one of the readings at Peter's memorial service.

I leaned forward and whispered to the nearest flight attendant, "Please tell my family that I love them very much". She shushed me, but I was sure that she had heard and with any luck would pass the message on. I felt better for that.

Because I felt better, I decided to say goodbye to everyone. I could not pass a message to them all, but in my mind I went around all the people I would miss and who would miss me. My sisters. My girlfriend. Old friends getting married in a few weeks, with me supposed to be the best man – sorry. Other friends, one by one, called to mind, goodbye. Today, I could not do this. I have a wife and two daughters: the thought that I would not see my daughters grow up, would not be there to help my wife bring them up, would not be able to grow old with the ones I love, would destroy me. I do not know what I would do. I just have to hope that I never have the opportunity to find out. I believe that this is one strong element of the suffering of all hostages: knowing that you may never see the ones you love again, may never get the chance to tell them. Part of the poem I recited for Pete at the foot of Broad Peak goes:

> *I never will again hold back on love:*
> *Love's object may not stay to share tomorrow,*
> *Life, like a welcome guest, too soon departing.*

I wrote it in 1983, but I did not live up to it in the meantime, and probably still don't today. But I am closer to it.

Of course, September 11 2001 was full of emotion for everyone who saw the newsreels and read the accounts. I would not say that ex-hostages felt any more than anyone else, although plenty of people have suggested to me that "I must". I think it may have been *different* for us, not necessarily *worse*. The thing that brought a lump to my throat more than anything else was the terrorists on United flight 93, apparently telling the passengers to phone their loved ones because they were going to die.

In the newspaper account I read, this was presented as the terrorists taunting the passengers. It may have been so: but to me, it would have been the thing in the world I would most want to do, to have a chance to say goodbye. The phone call would be awful, heart-ripping, but it would be better than disappearing into nothing without a word. To me, this was in effect – if not in intention – an act of humanity by people carrying out an inhuman act. It led to the crashing of the plane in "the wrong place", so it effectively cost them the success of their mission (unfortunately, this means that such "humanity" is unlikely to happen again – well, I hope that *none* of what happened that day ever happens again).

As I did the rounds, I went through the members of the expedition, and came to two I had not got along with all the time. I thought of the saying, "don't let the sun go down on your anger". I used to think it was like "the sun never set on the British Empire" – but now I could see its true meaning, and I tried to put our differences to rest for my part. The sort of arguments you have because you are cooped up with someone in a tent, or in the confines of Base Camp, are not very significant when you are about to die. I hoped that they might feel the same.

Eventually my thoughts turned to the hijackers. This is a point at which some people will think I lost the plot, but I decided that anger and the sun applied to them too. I did not want to die angry or frightened. This was not a religious thing: it was not about giving myself up to a mortal sin without hope of redemption. I just felt that I would like to die in peace, with dignity. So I determined that I would not hate them. I suppose I am a product of the comics I read as a boy – the *Eagle* and the *Boys' Own Paper* – and am a sucker for particular types of film. If Abbas had come down the stairs and said, "I'm going to shoot you now", I was determined to be all British-Empire-pith-helmet-and-stiff-upper-lip, and offer to shake his hand.

"All right; you have your reasons; do a clean job; I forgive you."

This is a load of rubbish, really. I probably couldn't have actually done it. I would have gibbered and begged for my life, just like poor Rajesh Kumar. Knowing, as I do now, how Abbas treated Kumar, he probably wouldn't have let me shake his hand anyway.

Because it never came to it, I was able always to believe that I would do it. Through the rest of the day, I wasn't really frightened of Abbas. He looked quite professional; if he decided to shoot me, he would probably shoot me dead outright, and there would be an end. I was absolutely certain that this would happen, and there was absolutely nothing I could do about it. All I had to do was to wait, and try to keep hold of my self-respect and my dignity. They weren't taking them away from me.

Jumbo on the taxiway at Karachi Airport

View of the plane from the control tower

Negotiators at work in the control tower

The front of the plane during the siege

The front steps -
afterwards

Fake security van used to gain
entry to the airport

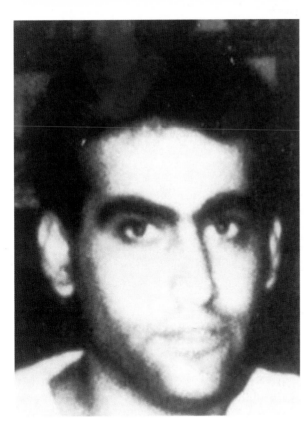

The man I knew as Abbas –
Zaid Hassan Abd Latif
Safarini

The first victim, Rajesh
Kumar – not an obvious
target, just the nearest body

Pan Am cabin crew course, early 1986 – eight out of fifteen were together on board on 5 September (Sunshine is third from left, Neerja is ninth)

Neerja Bhanot, the senior purser

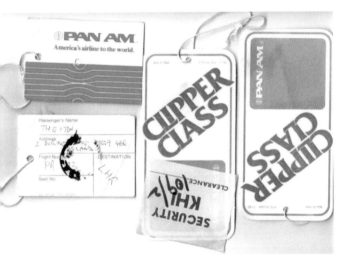

Cleared for take-off?
Security tags applied to
my hand luggage in the
airport

Not cleared for take-
off: some of the
terrorists' arsenal

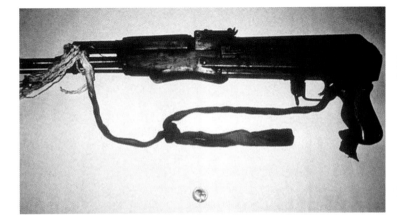

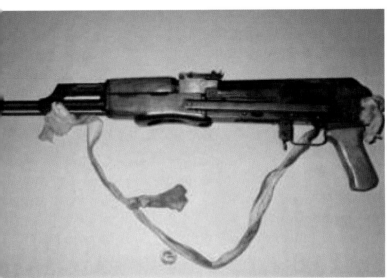

Two
Kalashnikov
AK-47s

More of the
terrorists'
weapons

Two handguns
with magazines

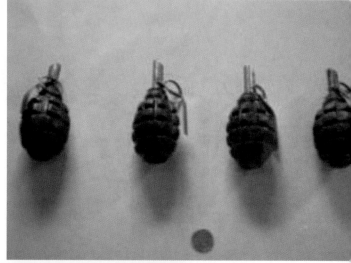

Hand grenades – at least
six were thrown in the
plane

Plastic explosive
worn by Abbas
around his waist

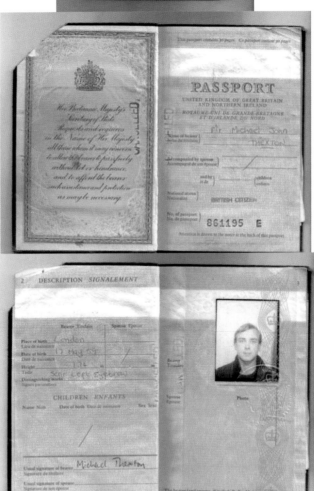

The second most unpopular passport in the world?

Where are the pilots? The spiral staircase, viewed from the front of the plane

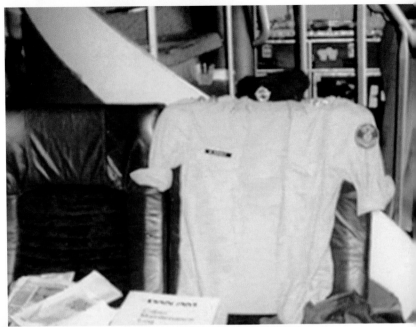

This is the space behind door L1 where I spent most of the day waiting to be shot– the flight attendants sat in the two pairs of seats aft of the door

Apart from saying goodbye, I said prayers. Back in the 1970s, when I went to college, British university education was free, and you even received a maintenance grant from the State to pay for beer. As it was free, my generation studied anything, without – in many cases (or perhaps it was just me) – much regard for what would happen afterwards. So it was that I have a degree in theology, without ever having intended to be a priest; by the end of my theology course, I was no longer the keen practising Christian I had been at the beginning. I suppose I had thought about the unprovability of everything for so long that my faith had not been strong enough to survive. Possibly I had just not read enough books.

Anyway, I could suggest a much better question for the final degree exam in theology than the one I actually sat:

You are being held at gunpoint and you expect to be shot later. You do not believe in God or in the power of prayer to achieve anything. Do you pray, and if so, why? (3 hours)

The answer to the first question was, "Yes, definitely". The answer as to "why" remains uncertain. As I knelt there and started to think about a prayer, I saw many things with extreme clarity. The first was that, if there was a God, He would know that I didn't believe in Him. So there wasn't any point trying to fool Him that I did. The next was that I was surely going to make some promises; but whatever I could promise was nothing in comparison with my life. It would be a bit like turning up on the doorstep of someone you haven't bothered to keep up with for five years and asking them suddenly for a loan.

He would also know whether I intended – whether I was able – to keep the promises. I could see myself marching up to the Pearly Gates in half an hour's time, looking around in mild surprise that it all really did look like some old film, with St Peter (wings and all) tapping a long finger on the ledger where my recent promises would be recorded and muttering, "You lying so-and-so, you didn't mean a single word of that, did you? Take the down escalator on the left."

So I said my prayers and made my promises: three of them. I didn't promise to believe in God, or to go to church every day for the rest of my life. I don't think I could or would have kept those promises, so I didn't make them. The details are personal, and so I will leave the nature of the promises as an exercise for the reader – a supplementary question in the above examination. What would you promise? It has to be serious, it has to matter; you have to be sure that you mean it; you have to go away afterwards and do it. You don't want to meet St Peter thirty minutes or sixty years later and find that you have short-changed the Almighty for your life.

As I knelt there saying my prayers, an idea came into my head that my parents believe was an immediate answer, a divine inspiration. My parents are more religious than me, which is just as well, as my father is a retired Methodist minister. It occurred to me that these men were Muslims – whether they were Pakistani, which was still possible, or Arab, which I was increasingly inclined to suspect. I was kneeling on the floor. I had my hands on my head rather than on my thighs, but I was not far from the position I had seen our mountain guide adopt when praying to Mecca. So I started to touch my head to the floor, straighten up, touch my head, straighten up. I don't know how long I could keep that up today – it's pretty strenuous. I suppose I was lean and fit and there was nothing else to do; it was somehow comforting.

The odd thing is that I cannot really say what I intended by it. It is a shocking admission that I had managed to go through a whole theology degree without doing a paper in comparative religion, and my knowledge of Islam was as rudimentary as the average westerner's. If they had asked me the simplest question, I could not have begun to persuade them that I was a real Muslim. There had been a Koran in the hotel room the previous night – the equivalent of a Gideon's Bible – and I could wish that I had read some of it. But it was too late for all that.

I heard indirectly that the flight attendants believed these actions saved my life. They saw the attitude of the hijackers change towards me. It may be that they thought I was a Muslim; it may merely be that I stopped being just "one body", and became more of a person. It's harder to shoot a person (although they were certainly capable of it).

Settling down to wait

I spent the rest of the day – perhaps twelve hours or so – at the front of the plane. During that time, not much happened – I waited to be shot, and the crisis never came. I will relate the incidents that punctuated the time, but I cannot really describe the bits in between – it is very strange to sit and think about nothing at all. I doubt if you can remove "tomorrow" from your mind unless you are sure that tomorrow will not come, and fortunately very few people are in that situation on a normal day. Many people will go through their whole lives without ever having the experience, even on the day before the tomorrow that does not come. For sure, most people will spend odd instants thinking that they are about to die, or a few minutes, but to sit and believe it for twelve hours is very peculiar.

I can only begin to imagine what it is like for a week, a month, five years. Adjusting back to *not* believing it was quite difficult for me, after even such a short time.

I remember hearing voices upstairs, and I guessed (correctly) that Abbas had started negotiating on the radio. Throughout the day I heard this several times, but I never had any idea what he was asking for or threatening. His voice was indistinct, the replies were inaudible, and in any case I am sure that they were speaking in Arabic. Even I had given up my attempts to understand foreign languages by this time.

I stole glances at the man who was now guarding me, and saw that he was younger – a teenager, maybe 17. He seemed to be the dogsbody of the team, and – probably as a result of that – was the most outwardly aggressive. The name I remember from the day is Ali, although the flight attendants understood that he was called Ismail. As with Mustafa/Abbas, neither is his real name. He had an acne-scarred face, and at different times carried a pistol and a Kalashnikov.

After a long time praying, both mentally and physically, I paused and tried to find something else to occupy my mind. Right beside me was a large pile of passports, with my passport on the top. Just for something to do, I picked up another from the pile and looked at it –

another Brit, D.A.Wilson. I remember thinking, "What's wrong with him, then?"

Ali pointed the gun at me and barked, "What you doing?"

I put the passport down, shrugged, put my hands back on my head and said, "Nothing".

He barked again, "Where you from?"

"I'm from London. Where are you from?"

"NOT YOUR BUSINESS!" I knew that, but it's hard to get out of the habits of polite conversation.

A bit later, Ali pointed the gun at me again, and stated, "You like thojja".

"Pardon?"

"You like thojja!"

"I'm sorry, I don't understand."

"YOU – LIKE – MOGGRET – THOJJA!" Ah – a political opinion poll!

"No! Not at all. I hate her."

He raised the gun with his arm straight out – straight arm and straight face – and asked me, "Why not?"

Well, where do you begin? I probably should have said, "Because she recently allowed the great Satan Ronald Reagan to bomb the blessed Colonel Gadaffy", which might have gone down well; but I actually came up with a party political broadcast on behalf of the Liberals – something along the lines of her being too hard on ordinary people, never listening. This seemed to be a moderately satisfactory answer, so he went back to passive scowling for a while.

I was not particularly afraid of Abbas once I had determined that he would shoot me, but I was afraid of Ali. He looked as though he was not entirely in control of himself; he might shoot me in the leg just for fun, and that would hurt. Someone who apparently has some training and discipline is easier to be around than someone who does not.

After maybe two hours of negotiating upstairs, Abbas came down again. He stopped beside me, looked down and asked, "You all right? You want a drink, some beer, some whisky?"

I wondered whether this was a test: a good Muslim would refuse alcohol. I decided to keep it going if possible, so I replied, "Maybe a 7-Up or some water, thank you".

He turned to the flight attendants and said, "Bring him a drink".

One of them stood up and asked, "May we take drinks to all the passengers?"

He considered this for a moment, then nodded. "Make an announcement: everyone must stay in their seats, and you can take drinks to all the passengers." At this stage of the day he seemed quite calm, even cheerful, and did not appear to want to make the passengers suffer more than their temporary imprisonment.

The cabin crew members went off to serve drinks. During the day, they took round more drinks, sandwiches, and later coffee. Each time, they brought extra back for me. At one point, they presented me with a large plateful of slightly dried-out sandwiches and a packet of roasted almonds. They say that the condemned man eats a hearty breakfast: all I can say is that it probably isn't Pan Am sandwiches. I didn't feel particularly hungry anyway, even though I had not had anything significant to eat since the previous day at lunchtime. I was used to getting by on not very much.

At one point, the attendants were away in the economy cabin, and Abbas came and sat in the seat opposite me. I remained on the floor throughout. He looked out of the window, the rifle across his lap, and I did not think of jumping him. Then he turned to me and asked, "Are you married?"

"No – I have a girlfriend, but I am not married."

"Oh." A pause – then, "I am sorry for this. I do not like this fighting, this killing. I would like to go out dancing, go out drinking, go out with women – but the Americans and Israelis have stolen my country, and without my country, these things are no good."

"Oh – so you're Palestinian, then?"

"Palestinian, yes."

Then he carried on looking out of the window. I wasn't going to speak unless spoken to, so I didn't try to continue the conversation any further. As far as I know, this was about the limit of their explanations of their cause to any of the passengers. I don't know why Abbas went that far with me – he never tried to justify his actions any further, and certainly never appeared to expect or require any co-operation from me. Maybe it was what it seemed to be at face value – he just felt the need to explain himself to me.

If that was the case, I had moved another step away from being "one body", and it was becoming harder to shoot me.

I have had other thoughts about this conversation in the years since the hijack. Sitting on the floor at Abbas' feet, I simply thought that it was sad that he had been driven to this by his sense of injustice. Waiting for him to kill me, but unaware that he had yet killed anyone else – I felt sorry for him. I felt that there was a difference between a man who thought that he was fighting for a just cause against an oppressor, and a madman who simply liked murder. However, I had no sympathy for his actions. What he was doing was clearly and terribly wrong; whether his cause was just or not, this would diminish the justice of it. It was not only wrong, it was a mistake, and therefore doubly tragic.

Of course, Abbas could have wanted me to believe that he was an honourable freedom fighter. He could have been really keen on murder and mayhem, but it suited him to put across the appearance of a reasonable man driven to desperate means. I am not sure that he was actually that clever, but it is possible. Pity the poor negotiator, who has to try to bargain with the man, not usually even able to see him – forming crucial judgements on the hijacker's state of mind can't be easy. After all, the hijacker may have been on a training course, just as the negotiator has. The terrorist may know how to create a false impression.

Alone at the front

At various points during the day, I was left alone. Abbas was aft or upstairs, and Ali was wherever Abbas was not; the flight attendants were serving passengers. The second-in-command was generally visible, standing in the doorway at the back of the business class cabin, but he was usually facing the other passengers in economy. I stayed on the floor beside the pile of passports. I never dared to promote myself into a seat. I knelt, sat and lay on the floor. You have no idea how comfortable even the economy class seats are until you have sat on the floor for a while – particularly without the benefit of the usual padding on the backside. There was not a great deal of flesh separating my bones from the hard plastic.

I could tell, just by looking at it, that the pile of passports did not contain any Americans. I did not realise that they had already been separated out, gone through and rejected. I assumed that, somehow, no Americans had handed their passports in. I was sure the people sitting next to me were Americans, and they had avoided it. I wondered if there had been some programme on ABC or NBC telling people what to do in a hijack, and why had the BBC not shown it with all the other imported American stuff? But I did not investigate the passports in any more detail after Ali had told me off.

The first time I was left alone, I was suddenly aware of a soft whimpering, coming from somewhere forward of my exit. I looked aft to where the terrorist in the doorway was looking the other way; the noise continued. I decided to investigate, but I was not sure that I should stand up – that might look like a "sudden movement". So I crawled up the aisle on my hands and knees, looking in between the first class seats. Just a few rows forward, a small Indian girl was crouched, crying. She was perhaps six years old. Her parents must have hidden her under a seat when they were sent back, and told her to wait there. She must have heard the bargaining over Kumar, and heard him shot.

I didn't know that, but I didn't think she could take much more of being alone in that scary place, so I held out a hand to her, and she came. I crawled backwards to the space by the doorway, holding her hand. Then I called to the terrorist, who turned to look. He showed no particular surprise at the sight of the child, but sent one of the flight attendants forward to collect her. I presume that she was reunited with her parents. I did not see her again, and I do not know what became of her.

Once when I was alone, I needed to use the toilet. There was a toilet block just aft of my exit door, but I did not want to seem to disappear. The first time I had needed to go, Abbas was there, and he frisked me before I went in (hard to imagine what I could have conjured from thin air in order to smuggle into the toilet – or why I would have wanted to smuggle anything in there – but he was clearly very wary of me). Now that I was on my own, I called out to the man in the doorway and made some basic gestures to indicate what I wanted. He waved a hand to say I could go. I went in and out as fast as possible, opening the door slowly to make sure I didn't bash into anyone.

On one occasion, he appeared to send one of the flight attendants forward to bring me a drink. He made a gesture as if to ask if I was all right, to which I raised my plastic cup of lemonade in acknowledgement. Never better! As far as I can remember, he never came forward of that doorway in the whole day.

So, there were several periods – spread out through the day, some short, some longer – when I was left alone by the exit door. Just me, my thoughts, and the door. The door, the lever, the red arrow showing how you swing it up and across. I had not read the emergency leaflet – being paranoid and obsessive, I used to do so even before the hijack, but we just hadn't got that far in the flight – but I knew how to open the door. I was absolutely sure that they would shoot me later, but I still never came within a mile of trying to escape. I can't explain that (apart from the possibility of rank cowardice). I suppose it's a bit like toothache (only worse): logic tells you that you need to pull the tooth out, but actually doing it can take a lot of getting around to.

Strangely, it appears to have been the right decision, even though it would have been hard to justify logically at the time. If people were going to be shot, they would surely include me, and I could not foresee any outcome where no-one would get shot; I was not going to go home any other way than by standing up and opening that door, and jumping... how far? Would the chute come down? Would I break a leg and be an easy target, sprawled and immobile on the runway? How long would it take me to open the door, and how long for the chute to inflate, and how long to get to the bottom? All those doubts gave me excuses not to try it.

There was another thought, which was probably me trying to make something noble out of my lack of bottle. I thought it very likely that my escaping would lead immediately to someone else being shot. I did not want to have to live with that, although I expect I would have managed it.

I also thought about the Americans I had been sitting next to... there were no American passports in the pile... surely they were after Americans... maybe, if I said something... no, I couldn't live with that either. Also, I wasn't sure that shopping someone else would actually do me any good. I'm sure it was the noble reason, though, that kept my mouth shut.

I didn't think of escaping, but I did form a plan for a storming. I knew that this was a possibility, although I had no idea how likely it was. I didn't know whether the Americans would come – the "US troops" Abbas had told the station chief to keep away – or possibly the SAS. In fact, we would have had the Pakistani commandos rather than either of the western armies. My plan was quite rudimentary. If the storming happened at the back of the plane, I would grab a fire extinguisher from a rack close by and try to jam myself under the seats in front with the metal cylinder providing some sort of protection.

If the storming happened at the front, I didn't really have a plan.

I thought about storming, and I thought about what else might be happening outside. I had very little idea of the politics of such a situation. I wasn't even sure whether Pakistan was part of the British Commonwealth at the time (it wasn't), but I was aware that Pakistan was a close ally of the USA because of the Afghan war going on beyond its north-west borders (how times change – the Islamic mujihadeen were then the good guys from the Americans' point of view, because they were beating up the Russians). I thought about General Zia ul-Haq, Ronald Reagan and Margaret Thatcher, three hard men – well, *two* hard men, but Zia and Thatcher would probably put some backbone into Ronald. They weren't going to give the terrorists what they wanted in order to get me out of here.

I thought about this, and believed very strongly that it was right. If these men got what they wanted – whatever it was, because they still hadn't seen fit to share the point of the exercise with us – then someone else would be kneeling behind an airplane door next week, and the week after, and the week after that. Eventually it would be my turn again. Better for them not to get what they want, and then maybe they won't bother another time. It doesn't work quite as well as that – people find different reasons to hijack planes – but I'm sure it works the other way around. If terrorists' demands are met, then it's a no-brainer – you get more terrorism.

I don't suppose I would have refused to leave the plane if, contrary to all expectation, Mrs Thatcher had announced that she would meet all the terrorists' demands in order for me to be released. But it would not have improved my opinion of her.

A little more conversation

At one point during the afternoon, there was almost a party atmosphere at the front of the plane. Abbas was sitting in one of the four seats, with four flight attendants around him. I was still on the floor – I knew my place. Abbas was doing his best with the women, telling them how brave and beautiful they were. They were doing their best to look brave and beautiful and not tell him what they thought of him. He said it was his birthday – he was 24. I asked (quietly) if we could have a going-home present at the end of the party.

Then the man in the shalwar-kameez walked up the aisle. I could see him coming because I was facing back down the plane. He was smoking a cigarette and holding a grenade in one hand. When he reached us, he showed me the grenade – apparently he had waved it under the nose of most of the passengers aft, and maybe he needed to show it to everyone to get his terrorism badge. He showed me that he had taken the pin out and had it in his fingers with the cigarette. He said nothing at all, but glanced – slightly disapprovingly? – at Abbas sitting with the flight attendants.

This is the closest I have ever been to a hand-grenade and the closest I ever care to be. I did not know exactly how they work, but I am told that there is a spring-loaded lever which is held in place by the pin. Once the pin is out, the lever can be held down by the thumb. If it is released, the spring ejects the lever and you can't put it back. A few seconds later, it will explode.

The grenade-man's silent message to each passenger was, "If you try anything with me, I will drop this, and we are both dead – but I don't care". There is not much you can do about him.

A few months later, back in normal life, I was slumped in front of the television surfing the channels late at night... it would be nice to be able to say that everything in my life afterwards was full of significance and purpose, but that doesn't last for long. I came across a made-for-TV movie about a hijack. I was too stunned to turn over and I watched it in the same way that a rabbit might watch the approaching headlights – stupefied horror. The thing was, they had a grenade-man, wandering up and down the cabin with the pin between his teeth, and I just had to know: what were they going to do about him? In the end, of course, the passengers leapt on him so quickly that they managed to get their hands around his fist and hold on so tight that he couldn't drop the grenade. Then they got the pin back in. It was the funniest thing I'd ever seen. "Don't try this at home", as they used to say at the end of Batman.

Back on the plane, the man turned on his heel and walked back – but only as far as the toilet, a few paces behind where everyone was sitting. As he went inside, I wondered, "What's he going to do with the grenade...?" I had an incongruous mental picture of him tucking it between his legs.

DERRRR DERRRR DERRRR DERRRR

Suddenly a siren blared out. Party over, Abbas jumped to his feet, pointing his gun this way and that, shouting, "What is happening, what is happening?" He was obviously expecting to see men in balaclavas coming through the walls. I demonstrated the civilian reaction again in failing dismally to disappear under a seat with my fire extinguisher.

One of the flight attendants coolly stood up and held up a hand to calm Abbas down. "It's all right, he's smoking in the toilet – it's the fire alarm." She took three steps down the aisle, opened the door with an external release handle, then averted her eyes from whatever she could see, said "Excuse me", and reached up to turn off the alarm. Then she serenely walked back and took her seat. It was a magnificent display of grace under pressure.

The whole episode – half a minute long – was quite comic. But it could have been an absolute disaster. Apart from anything else, the man in the toilet could have dropped his grenade. Abbas could have opened fire on a shadow and, if he had, the other terrorists would have started shooting as well.

The poor negotiator is sitting in the control tower on chai-break, feeling relaxed, everything going well, no deadlines for a while – and they're shooting the passengers! What's going on? The problem is that you can predict that something unpredictable will happen, but you cannot predict what it will be, or when it will be. Since September 11, the most predictable spanner in the works is a hostage having a go at the hijackers, just when everything has reached a peaceful conclusion and they are about to give up.

At another point, I was lying on the floor, half asleep. Ali was talking to the flight attendants. Unlike Abbas, he did not seem to want to flirt – he was giving them a lecture: "I hate rich people. Rich people kill our children. I hate the Americans. I hate the British. I hate the French. I hate the Spanish." I lay on the floor thinking, "Who hates the Spanish? The Spanish are nice people" (revealing again my dismal lack of knowledge of the history of Spain and Islam, but never mind).

So, Ali hated rich people, and the flight attendants sat and listened to his lecture. It only struck me years later that the terrorists really were having a bad day. No flight crew; cabin crew are Indians; most of the passengers are clearly Indian and Pakistani; the American passports all have brown faces; so we'll have a Brit – and the Brit turns out to look like the most pitiful refugee. I think now that they didn't know what to make of me. They wanted a nice rich enemy in a suit, and they got an bearded weirdo in a red duvet jacket, clearly worse fed than any of them.

Perhaps there is a God after all. He thought, "Let them pick Thexton. They won't shoot him."

Beginning of the end

I am not sure of the time, but other stories suggest about six o'clock in the evening for the next event. I was again half-asleep in the space behind my door, and I was disturbed by a noise in the centre of the plane. I sat up and saw two of the flight attendants opening a hatch in the floor, just forward of the spiral staircase. A moment later Abbas came clattering down the stairs and asked what they were doing.

One of the crew members looked up from her crouching position on the floor. "We are getting out the medical equipment. We have a sick passenger, and we have found a doctor. We are just getting the medical equipment."

Abbas, now standing over them at the foot of the stairs, simply said, "Put it back".

The woman looked puzzled. "But we need the medical equipment for a sick passenger…".

Abbas stayed completely calm, but he held out a hand, palm down, and lowered it to emphasise the point. "Put it back."

At this, she realised what was going on – rather quicker than I did – and stood up, put an angry finger in Abbas' face and scolded him: "You are a very bad man. You cannot do this to these people, these people have done nothing to you. You must let us take the medical equipment for this sick passenger."

He simply repeated the gesture with his hand, and said again, "Put it back".

The flight attendant had little choice but to compose herself, close the hatch, speak softly to her colleague and go aft to explain the position to the doctor and the passenger.

I sat there thinking, "That's funny, he's been perfectly reasonable all day. Why won't he let them treat a sick passenger?" Perfectly reasonable, of course, for someone who has been holding us all at gunpoint and is certain to shoot me later. But he had not, up to that point, done anything quite so pointedly cruel – not in my sight, anyway – as refusing treatment for a sick passenger. My standards of what constituted reasonable behaviour had slipped slightly.

Once again, I come up against the same difficult question: was he a reasonable man who was prepared to be brutal in order to achieve his ends, or a brutal man who was prepared to appear reasonable for the same purpose? I couldn't tell, and I was probably better placed than most. The records of his conversations with the control tower include the threat: "We will not spare anybody in the plane, whether young or old, if you do not co-operate. We will not leave anyone. We are merciless people, we do not know tolerance."

The point, which I did not realise until much later, is that a sick passenger is a good extra bargaining counter. Abbas did not want to sit here for a week. If he had, he would almost certainly have got rid of the women and children, the old and the sick – as well as riff-raff like me, in all probability. He would have tried to identify a few high ranking hostages – the US aid official, the oil company executive, the international bank auditor, a few others – and so make the situation much more manageable. If you have ten valuable people you can guard them, feed them, allow the toilets to cope. Your men can rest as you take watches. Abbas wanted to turn the screw, force a resolution. As the chief bargaining counter, I should have been feeling more nervous than I was.

*****

Later still, I was asleep again, when I was abruptly woken by Ali kicking my feet. This was the only physically rough treatment that I received in the whole day and it was hardly severe – I was still wearing my mountaineering boots and Ali probably hurt his toes. He said, "Up, move!", waving a gun at me. I picked myself up, put my hands in the air and stumbled half-asleep down the aisle again.

It struck me that it was darker, quieter and hotter: it seemed that night was falling, but that made no sense inside the plane. Thinking about it afterwards, I could tell that the electrical systems were failing – the air conditioning had stopped and the muzak was gone, so it was nearly silent; the temperature was rising because of the lack of air, and the lights were dimming noticeably. The auxiliary power unit that supplies the electricity on the ground had run out of fuel, or broken down, after running for a full twelve hours – much longer than it would ever normally have to – and the batteries were rapidly becoming exhausted.

Apparently one of the flight attendants had shortly before this made an announcement to the rest of the passengers that the authorities were going to bring out a generator to restore power, but this generator never came. One of the things that went with the rest of the electrics was the cockpit radio, so communications were cut off. The chief negotiator, director of civil aviation Air Vice-Marshal Mirza Khan, came down from the control tower and went out to the plane with a megaphone, but the doors were shut.

This could have been predicted and it could have been dealt with, but it was not.

I walked through the doorway into the forward economy cabin, and found it exactly as I had left it – full of scared people. During the day, looking down the aisle and seeing some movement in the cabin, I had believed that maybe they were letting women and children off – but it was obviously not so. There were still people sitting on the floor. I looked for somewhere to go.

Here, I was very lucky. Unknown to me, there had been seven passengers upstairs all day, together with the ground crewman Kharas. They, together with the flight attendants from the front, had walked down the aisle a moment earlier – perhaps Ali had noticed me lying quietly in the doorway and rounded me up almost as an afterthought. Everyone was being brought together in one place. When the others walked through the doorway, most of the seats in the front row were empty, and they sat there. Many of them died or were badly injured. They were right in front of the guns when the shooting started.

When I came through the door, the front row was full, so I kept walking. I think someone must have taken my earlier aisle seat next to the North American couple (probably cursing the big green bag under their feet), but I saw another pair of empty seats in the starboard bank of three, a few rows in front of the wing exit. There was a man sitting by the aisle, so I stepped over him and took the window seat. A mixture of fear and hope gripped me. I was back with the others – I stood a chance. But something was about to happen – the tension in the air left no-one in any doubt.

I could see that the man in the shalwar-kameez had gone to the front of this cabin on the starboard side, now armed with a gun as well as a grenade. Abbas was level with him on the port side, by the door through which I had come back from business class. The lights went lower and lower, leaving only a glimmer of pinpoints which showed shapes rather than any detail. I crouched as low as I could get in the seat, which was a lot lower than it would have been if I had still had my green bag in front of me. The terrorists called to each other in their own language, but in between their shouts the cabin was silent – so quiet that it was possible to hear someone snoring gently in the middle block of seats. The silence lengthened…

BANG

I remember thinking, "Is that a hand grenade? Surely a grenade would be deafening in here." But the bang was quite quiet, like a small firework. A moment later, there was automatic gunfire coming from the front of the cabin, loud and unmistakeable. I must have been six or seven rows back – maybe twenty feet – from where Abbas was firing his Kalashnikov, emptying the magazines one after another. Then there was more automatic fire from the rear of the plane, sounding as if it was in a different country – the distance is so great and the plane is constructed to absorb sound. Then there was more gunfire from the front, and more from the back.

Afterwards, the plane showed the evidence of at least six grenade-blasts, two in each cabin. The hijackers methodically threw their bombs into the passengers. I only remember hearing one. Perhaps the bangs were lost in the gunfire, or maybe they were so loud they blanked my memory. Two of them were very close to where I was sitting at this point, at the left-hand end of the centre seating blocks in rows 25 and 28. I was in the window seat on the same side of the plane, somewhere between row 23 and 27. I don't know how I was untouched by the blasts.

The people in front of the guns had no chance at all. Just a few rows back, we were protected by rows of seats – built to take the impact of a crash landing, as well as to deaden sound – and those seats had bodies in them as well. The bullets did not reach as far as me.

In the block of seats in the middle of the plane, a mother was sitting with her three year old son and two year old daughter. As the lights went down, she whispered to them, "Please don't make any noise, they will kill us". As the shooting started, she pushed them down onto the floor and tried to cover them with her body. In the darkness, she could feel something warm, wet and sticky on them, and asked them desperately if they were hurt. They were not, but they knew that they must not speak or the bad men would kill them: they kept quiet. In the dark and the panic, the woman had no way of knowing that it was the blood of one of the passengers in the seats around her, not her children's blood. She could only be sure once she had picked them up, one under each arm, run to the exit behind her and climbed out onto the wing.

An American man had spent the day next to the starboard wing door, R3. When the shooting started, he leaned over to a cabin crew member sitting beside him and whispered, "Open the door" – no reaction. He tried again, a little louder, "Open the door!" When the crew member still didn't move, the passenger shouted "OPEN THE GODDAMN DOOR", and then decided to do it himself. As he stood up and took hold of the handle, a bullet hit the door right in front of his face. He was out of it quite quickly after that.

Catherine Hill, an English woman returning from travelling around India with her Italian boyfriend, was sitting in the rear section of the plane near door R4. A grenade went off in the aisle right by her seat, blowing her left buttock off. She felt the blood running out of her, but did not have the relief of losing consciousness. Her boyfriend saw that the door was open and the chute was deployed; he picked her up and threw her out of the plane, following her down. In spite of shrapnel injuries to his own feet, he carried and dragged her across the runways away from the plane, fearing that it might explode at any moment. They found no help until they reached the perimeter. There, two men and a pick-up truck took them to a hospital.

Sunshine had come back from the front of the plane with Abbas, Kharas, the other cabin crew members and the passengers from upstairs. Abbas ordered her to go further back down the plane. She went back to the area by the port wing door (L3), and he waved at her to go further back. She looked around to see where her colleagues were – Neerja and one of the others were by Abbas at the L2 door; there were three more cabin crew members crouched in the centre of the plane between the lavatories, and at least one more on the far side by the R3 door. She decided that she would be of most use by the L3 door – she too felt that something was about to happen, and if there was a stampede, she needed to be somewhere that she could help the passengers. She knew that the flight attendants at each door would do their best to get the exits open and help the passengers out.

When the shooting started, she kept her eyes open, needing to know what was happening. She saw the gunfire aimed first up in the air, then horizontally, then down. The people sitting in front of her in the aisle were hit, and she crouched down lower. Something lodged in her hair, probably a fragment chipped off the interior of the plane. She saw the flash and heard the crump of a grenade, and felt sharp nicks in her legs as small pieces of metal hit her. At the smell of smoke, she kept low, as she was trained to do in a fire.

Then she saw that the R3 door was open and people were moving towards it. The people around her needed no encouragement to go, so when the aisle was clear she followed them out to the door. She had seen one of the terrorists close to the L3 door and thought it would be too dangerous to try to open it.

Out on the wing, she found passengers – and some crew members – lining up to jump off the wing. Someone tried to pull her towards the edge, but she had no intention of leaving while she might be needed on the plane. Passengers saw her uniform and started screaming at her, demanding instructions, wanting help. She found a male flight attendant and told him to help calm the passengers down. She had to shout at them to try to shock them out of their panic.

She reckoned they could not jump off the wing safely – old people, children – and she could see that the chute was deployed on the R4 door, with people tumbling down it. So she went back to the doorway to see if it was safe to go back inside. People crowded behind her, following the uniform, and she had to stand in the doorway holding onto the handles on each side in order to keep them behind her. She took a look inside the cabin to make sure that the shooting had stopped. She thought that she would be young and fit enough to jump out of the way if someone threatened her; but she must have been silhouetted clearly against the sky behind her, and if the terrorists had had any ammunition left, she would surely have been shot. When no-one fired at her, she concluded that it was safe and stood aside to let people get in.

After the more able-bodied had climbed back up and into the plane, she realised that the step from the wing to the sill of the door was too much for some of the older passengers. Getting out and down had been easy, but up and in was beyond them. Sunshine climbed into the doorway and started pulling them up, while one of her colleagues pushed from behind. A mob formed around the door, and Sunshine had to shout and struggle to get them into some sort of order.

She did her best to control both the chaos and her own anger and frustration with the passengers. There were people out on the wings with their carry-on luggage (I can understand that). One man pushed his bag at her, trying to get her to take it inside the plane again. She lost patience, slapped him and threw the case off the wing.

The wings are sloping and smooth, and many people were in their socks – they had taken off their shoes to be more comfortable while sitting for all those hours on the plane. Sunshine saw people struggling with bags, slipping and tripping and losing their balance. Some ended up falling off the wings without getting themselves ready for the drop, landing any which way, on their backs, on their heads. That would hurt.

When she reckoned that everyone was off the wing in one direction or other, she ordered some of the men to help carry injured people towards the R4 door. She looked towards L2, where she had last seen Neerja, just in front of Abbas. There must have been a little light, because she saw Neerja moving. She ran to help her, but found she was covered in blood, trying to get up but collapsing back onto a seat. She tried to pick her up, calling to one of her colleagues for help, reassuring her that she would be all right, struggling to hold her because she was slippery with blood.

She felt someone grab her leg, looked down and thought she saw Abbas' face. She guessed he had been shot in the crossfire, kicked out at him and carried on trying to get a hold on Neerja. One of her male colleagues took Neerja's legs and together they carried her back to R4 and slid her down the chute. After a last look into the cabins to see if there was anyone else she could help, Sunshine jumped out.

From the wing, she had seen passengers running away from the plane with no-one to meet them, no ambulances, no security, no firemen, no commandos. Now, running from the plane, she finally found people on the ground to help. She directed them towards some of the injured passengers. At last, some security guards pushed her into an ambulance and drove her away in the direction of the terminal buildings.

I was hiding as low as I could get between the seats. After four bursts of firing, there seemed to be a pause, which seemed to extend into peace. Of course, it could not have been as silent as I remember it: people were dead and dying, wounded and crippled, and there must have been screaming and shouting. All I remember is raising my head far enough to see across to the other side of the plane. Everything was dark, but in my line of sight there was a different colour of black, and it was door-shaped. Someone had opened starboard door number three.

I reached out to the man in the aisle seat, who I could dimly see in the glimmer. "Come on, they're opening the doors, let's go." He put his hand on my head and pushed me back. "Keep down!" I had had enough at this point. There was a strong smell in the air, probably from the guns and grenades but possibly a fire. I knew that the plane would be fuelled up to fly to Frankfurt. I pushed back. "Come on, it's on fire. We've got to get out."

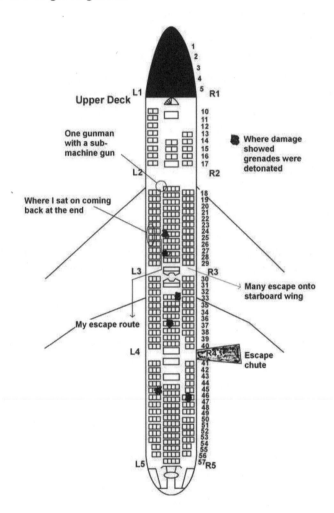

He seemed to take the point and I followed him out into the aisle, half-crouched, not knowing what danger there might still be. He started clambering through the seats to get to the other side, but I glanced back and saw that the nearest usable exit was behind me – port door number three was also open.

Looking back afterwards, I realised how lucky I was to be travelling alone. Two months with the group and suddenly cut loose: beyond the general human empathy with my neighbours, I had no particular reason to look out for anyone but myself at this point. I hope that it would have been different if I had had a wife and children around me, as some passengers did. I hope: I have no way of telling. I hope I never have to put it to the test.

I stepped over a man's body in the aisle. I do not know whether he was dead, or injured, or just keeping down. I have to say that I didn't much care. I must have been one of the first to move, because there was no crush at the door when I reached it. I stepped out into the night and found myself on the wing. There was no chute and no light – the terminal buildings were on the other side of the plane and in this direction the runways were just blank space.

There is a moment at the start of every flight that I now listen for carefully. When an aircraft is on the ground, a switch is turned on the emergency exits so that the chutes will not come down automatically. Otherwise the accidental opening of a door will delay the plane for hours while the chute is recovered and repacked. One of the last things you will hear before the plane goes forward onto the runway to take off is something like, "Flight attendants, doors to automatic and cross-check, take your seats for take-off". After that, opening a door will trigger the chute. On landing, you will hear, "Doors to manual". After that, you have to pull a separate handle to make the chute come down. The wing exits were opened by passengers, and the passengers didn't know that. The starboard number four door was opened by cabin crew, and the chute was deployed. But that was on the other side of the plane from me. Hardly anyone else came out of door L3, and L4 was not opened at this time. Nearly everyone else was getting out on the other side of the aircraft. I was on my own on the wing.

During the expedition, the others – proper climbers – despaired of my inability to jump over the smallest crevasse without a course of counselling before and after (and sometimes during). I had no idea how high a jumbo jet wing is, but I wanted to get off it quickly, so I decided the best plan was to slide on my front off the trailing edge, dangle a moment at the full extent of my arms, and then drop lightly what would surely be a few remaining feet to the ground. In fact, there is nothing to hold onto on the back of a jumbo jet wing (not many people can tell that from personal experience) and I went over the edge at some speed. It's also a long way down – I'm still not sure exactly how high, but I always look in wonder at 747s when I see them in an airport. It's something like jumping from the roof of a house – not out of the upstairs windows, but right off the top.

Here was another piece of luck. I was thirty-five pounds underweight, fitter than I had ever been, used to jumping about on rocks, and wearing a pair of mountaineering boots. Many of the injuries were from jumping off the wings, quite a few suffered by people jumping in their socks and bare feet after leaving their shoes behind in the stampede. I landed in a bit of a heap, but all I suffered was a scratch on the elbow. I picked myself up, took a quick look around – no-one in sight, everything dark – and headed for the nearest buildings, which were lit up not far away in front of the aircraft.

I ducked my head and zig-zagged as I ran, D-Day landing fashion. No-one was taking the blindest bit of notice, but I thought it's what I ought to do. I glanced round very briefly at the plane – it was a dark shape silhouetted against the slightly paler night sky. I recall hearing shots, but I don't know whether these were from inside or outside the plane.

There were some cars parked in front of the buildings – good cover for escaping bandits, but also cover for a small group of passengers and two flight attendants. One of them said, "Follow me!", so we did – through a gap in the buildings and into an enclosed courtyard. This was the stuff of horror movies – the bogeymen behind us, no way out. Someone in front opened a door and called, "In here". It was some sort of store-cupboard. I must have been the first in because I ended up crouched against the back wall, with one of the female flight attendants sitting on my feet, and – I think – another five people crammed in between her and the door.

The man by the door had a serious moustache. He announced proudly that he was with the Pakistani special forces and it would all be all right. I am not sure whether this was simply bravado – he didn't do anything more dramatic than close the door and lean on it while we all said "Ssshhhh!" to each other deafeningly.

The girl sitting on my feet half turned and said, "I am very sorry. I am pissing in my panties." I told her that she was welcome. I was in the strangest mental state – I was sure that I would wake up in a minute and find myself back on the plane. I could not believe that I had escaped. It was simply not possible, not credible.

We heard comings and goings outside the door, but we kept quiet. There were unidentifiable noises further off that might have been heavy vehicles. I imagined flares being fired up to illuminate the scene. Eventually – after perhaps half an hour, maybe more, it seemed like forever – someone came and banged on the door. We were not too keen to open it – not wanting at all to see someone in a security guard's uniform – but this turned out to be the real thing, and we stumbled out of our cupboard. We were led rapidly up some stairs, into the darkened building, through some offices and out onto the taxiway again. We boarded ambulances and were taken back to the departure lounge we had left that morning.

*****

I have been asked many times, "Why did they start shooting?" I don't know. Because it was part of their trial defence that they had been responding to a storming by commandos (I'll come back to that), they have never – as far as I know – explained why. There were suggestions from people who claimed to know some Arabic that they were shouting to each other as they took up their positions, "This is the final act!" But that could be for different reasons – they could have been egging each other on to carry out all their threats, or they could just have reckoned – like the rest of us – that the lights going out signified that something was going to happen.

A picture appeared afterwards in the press showing clearly the marks of two bullets in the outside of the cockpit windows. This remains unexplained. It appears that someone outside the plane attempted to shoot someone in the cockpit, but it's not clear when, why or with what result. I feel sure that if this had happened when any of the terrorists was still in the cockpit, they would have shot me immediately. I can't believe that these bullets prompted Abbas to calmly gather his hostages in the economy cabins, wait a bit and then start shooting. The response would have been immediate. So I expect that the snipers who must have had their sights trained on the cockpit all day, lying on the hot roofs of nearby buildings, heard the gunfire and decided to have a go at anyone who might have been in the darkened cockpit – but, in fact, there was no-one there. I think it's likely that the shooting at the cockpit followed on from the gunfire in the plane, rather than causing it.

So, why did they start shooting? It could be that they had concluded that they were getting nowhere and just decided that they would carry out their threat. But it seems that there was not an immediate deadline in prospect: if there had been, the commandos would surely have been closer. It could be that they thought they were under attack in the dark, and one of them panicked. As soon as one of them saw a shadow move and threw a hand-grenade at it, the others were all going to open fire. They themselves may not know. Some of them may actually believe that there were commandos storming the plane.

Whatever the reason, there is no way that they could justify a claim that they were resisting a commando attack. The firing and the grenades were aimed at the passengers, indiscriminately and without mercy. Whatever set them off, they all certainly and intentionally carried out the threats that Abbas had been making all day: "There will be many victims on the plane. The victims will be innocent children and women... the passengers will be the victims."

*****

That's it, really. A wise man – E.M. Forster? – said that all stories should finish with a separation, because that is a proper ending. Otherwise, you are forever tying up the loose ends. "They all lived happily ever after" is more of a beginning than a conclusion. But I will tell some of what happened afterwards, because some people may disagree with E.M. Forster.

AFTERMATH

The terminal

The ambulance dropped us by the doors to the terminal, and we passed back in through the plate glass barrier. Inside, there was a scene of chaos: I think we had probably missed the worst of it by hiding out in our cupboard, but most of the passengers – uninjured and walking wounded – had congregated in the departure lounge, where the security forces were holding them until they were sure that there were no terrorists among them. At least one – the grenade man – did try to mingle with the passengers, throwing off his shalwar-kameez and lying down on a bench in just his vest and underpants. He was spotted by a group of women and was plucked away by the security forces just as some quick and bloody justice was about to be meted out.

It seemed that there was no particular plan to deal with the sudden arrival of several hundred escaping passengers. I suppose that was quite unpredictable, but there was a plan in hand to storm the plane. If it had not ended when it did, it would certainly have ended three hours or so later. I don't know whether the strategy included some idea of what to do with the passengers, but that had not been worked out and communicated to the people in the departure lounge three hours before the storming was due.

The passengers walked up and down the room, greeting each other and expressing relief and congratulations. Several people came up to me and shook my hand – the couple I had sat next to at the beginning, the man covered in someone else's blood; the man I had sat next to at the end, who had left by the door on the other side of the plane; others who I had not been aware of, but who had seen me go forward. I found several of the flight attendants who had been sitting with me through the day. They all hugged me and said how pleased they were to see me. I had a particularly enthusiastic greeting from Sunshine – I thought it was just my animal magnetism, but I was unaware that she had been looking at me all afternoon in the knowledge that she had put me at the front of the queue.

There seemed to be no organisation, no official making decisions. I believe that, in fact, Air Vice-Marshal Mirza Khan was somewhere in the lounge giving instructions – but every single problem was being referred to him, and there was no overall plan and no delegation. If I walked towards the exits, there were people barring the way, keeping all the passengers within the lounge; but no-one seemed to know what was going to happen, or when we might be able to leave.

There were a few airport staff moving among the passengers. Someone was handing out cigarettes and I took one, thinking that this was a fine time to start smoking. It was pretty disgusting. There was a telephone on an official's desk, but apparently it wouldn't make an international call.

A westerner approached me, and said he was from *The New York Times*. Could I tell him what had gone on? I started to speak, but two uniformed Pakistani soldiers came up and told me not to talk to him. "Don't take any notice of them", he said – but I just told him that I had had a really difficult day and I didn't want any more bother. He growled in frustration and went off to look for someone else. The soldiers followed him – they obviously did not think they could throw him out, but they wanted to stop him getting any information.

After a while, I recognised the white-haired Englishman from the morning, and also Dennis Wilson, who I knew from his passport photograph. White-hair introduced himself as Ed Pomeroy, and congratulated me on my survival. He was probably in his mid-fifties and was clearly a seasoned business traveller – a bank auditor who spent his life in airports. He probably didn't often wander around them without any shoes, but he still seemed completely at home and in control of the situation. Dennis, maybe in his mid-thirties, was much more upset, but Ed seemed to have taken us both under his wing.

"Come on, we'll go to the Sheraton, send Pan Am the bill."

We moved towards the exits again, and on the way we met the British Vice-Consul – a man straight out of a Graham Greene novel, short and balding with sweat on his forehead and a tropical suit, rather hassled but doing his best. He took our details, noted that we intended to go to the Sheraton if we could get out of the airport, and introduced us to his young female assistant before hurrying off to find any other Britons who might be around. She told us that her colleagues would come and check on us later to make sure that we were all right.

We were in the terminal for perhaps an hour after escaping from the plane. I could now look at my watch again, but I don't recall doing so. Eventually, the authorities seemed to be allowing people to leave. They were checking people through several lines, asking who they were, taking down some details. Most of us had no identification, but Ed just said to the man that we were all British, and this was so obviously true from the way he said it that we were nodded past. We went out to the taxi rank and caught a cab into town.

*****

Meanwhile, some soldiers approached Sunshine and told her that they needed her to identify some hijackers that they had caught. They told her there was nothing to worry about, the hijackers would not see her; she said she was not scared. Then they took her to a room at the back of the terminal and pushed her in. They stayed outside. She was alone in a small room with Ali and the man who had spent the day by the L2 door between economy and business class. They looked at her, she looked at them; she stepped back outside and told the soldiers who they were. Then they took her to a truck outside where they were holding the grenade man, and she identified him as well.

As if this ordeal was not enough, they said that one of the hijackers was dead, and Sunshine was required to go to the hospital to identify him too. One of her male colleagues went with her. They drove 10 miles away to a hospital building where bodies were lined on benches, covered with sheets, eleven or twelve of them. They took her along the line, pulling back the sheets one by one. Only the men could have been the hijacker, but the soldiers did not bother to check first. They showed her everyone. The people who had been killed by grenades were a horrific sight. One of the sheets was pulled back to reveal Neerja, dead from her wounds.

Neerja was awarded the Star of India, her country's highest civil decoration, for her bravery. The fact that it was awarded posthumously still brings a lump to my throat after nineteen years.

Finally, they took Sunshine to the operating theatre. Someone had become suspicious of a wounded passenger on the table when they cut away his clothes and found a strip of plastic explosive around his waist. Sunshine had spent much of the day dealing directly with Abbas, and she was aware that he knew quite a lot about her; she did not want him to see her, to know that she had pointed the finger at him. But the officials simply pushed her in regardless. He was conscious and he saw her confirm that he was the leader of the gang. Satisfied, the officials left. Sunshine and her colleague had to wait at the hospital for an hour before someone took pity on them and drove them to a hotel.

The Sheraton

The Sheraton hotel is in downtown Karachi, so this was a longer journey than the previous night's bus-ride. Ed seemed in very good spirits. He told me that he and Dennis had sat together on the floor in one of the doorways throughout the day, and had passed the time playing cards. He reckoned Dennis owed him a considerable amount of money by now. Abbas had come past at one point and asked them what they were doing – he said they were playing Nap, and Abbas simply commented that he did not know the game. He had not seemed to mind that they were amusing themselves rather than sitting still.

Apparently he had then told them, "We will soon be going to the beach". This was about as close as anyone on the plane ever got to hearing what they were trying to achieve: the release of three Palestinian terrorists who had been convicted and imprisoned in Cyprus for the murder of three Israelis in a bomb attack on a yacht in Larnaca harbour in 1985. They hoped to fly the plane to Cyprus to carry on the negotiations there (or, at least, that was the story they presented to the negotiators: they might have actually done many other things if they had obtained a crew).

One of the convicted bombers they were trying to liberate was a man called Ian Davison, from South Shields in England. A few years later he was released and deported by the Cypriot authorities, and I saw his picture in the London Evening Standard on 1 October 1993. The story below it read:

PLO killer Ian Davison arrived back in Britain last night after being freed from a life sentence in Cyprus – and found he had nowhere to go. Hours earlier, he had been released under an amnesty and deported from the island after serving eight years for his part in murdering three Israelis. Davison, 35, a former carpenter from South Shields, Tyne & Wear, who said he was working for the PLO when the killings took place in 1985, passed through Heathrow with the minimum of formalities but waited several hours before leaving the arrivals area. There was no-one to greet him at the airport and he made several phone calls to locate friends in the London area. A policeman said: "We have not been questioning him. He is just trying to find somewhere to lay his head for the night."

I have no idea where he is now. I also have no idea why a Sandancer (I understand he cannot be correctly called a Geordie because he is from south of the Tyne) should be working for the PLO.

When we arrived at the hotel, we found the first evidence of forward planning that we had yet seen. There was a desk set up to receive people from the plane, and we were given rooms with the minimum of fuss and formality. It was fairly obvious where we came from, and no questions were asked about ID or payment (or luggage!). I left Ed and Dennis and went upstairs to find my room.

It was very strange finally to be alone. I have to admit that I looked under the bed and in the cupboards, and I put the chain on the door. I picked up the phone and asked the operator if he could put me through to my parents' number in England. He said he would try, but it might be some time, so I took the opportunity to have my second bath in a row (you wait two months for one, and then two come along at once).

By the time I had finished, the phone was ringing. I was surprised that the operator had managed the connection so quickly. My mother's voice sounded a little unsure – "Hello?"

"Hello, I'm just ringing to say that I'm all right. I don't know if you know that I might not be." I had never had time or chance to pass a message home about my changed flight, so there was no reason for them to think that I would have been involved.

She told me that my girlfriend, Louise, had seen the morning news – midday in Pakistan – and had immediately had a premonition that I was on board. Fortunately her intuition was not sufficiently detailed to know exactly what my situation was, but she rang the Foreign Office and they confirmed that I was one of the Britons on the passenger list.

My younger sister had been travelling in India with three college friends while I was in Pakistan, and she was due home that day – flying by Aeroflot from Bombay via Moscow. One of her friends rang the Foreign Office to ask if a Vicky Thexton was on the plane, and was told no, but there was a Michael Thexton. So my parents might have found out that way as well.

They had gone to Heathrow Airport to collect Vicky, and Louise rang them when they returned. She told my father that she had some really awful news, and he asked her what it was; when she said that I was aboard the hijacked plane, his first thought was apparently, "Is that all?" I suppose that it was less bad than the phone call about Peter in July 1983. While there is life – or no news of death – there is hope.

I spoke briefly to my mother, to Louise, to Vicky, and told them only that I was fine and would be coming home as soon as I could. I didn't tell them about my day, and they didn't tell me about theirs. Vicky had returned with two of her friends, about as thin as I was and ready for a celebration meal – complete with longed-for apple crumble (they had been having the same food fantasies in India that we had in the mountains, and had written ahead with requests) – that our mother had prepared. They ate it anyway, but the atmosphere was not quite there. They followed the news all afternoon. The BBC had led with the hijack on the six o'clock bulletin, and had closed with the flash that there was shooting aboard the plane. "We'll bring you more news in the nine o'clock programme." Two and a half hours would be a long time to wait for details.

My call probably arrived at about half past eight, UK time. After we hung up, Vicky – overcome by a stomach bug she brought home from India, exhaustion, and emotion – proceeded to be very sick all over the kitchen. My mother thought that this was just about the last straw.

Back in my hotel room, I did not feel like sleeping. I suppose it was partly the adrenalin rush of still being alive; partly the thought that I did not want to waste a second of this new life that had been given back to me; partly that I did not trust the cupboards to remain empty of terrorists if I took my eyes off them. So I turned on the television, and found they were showing "The Eiger Sanction". This is a film I have enjoyed on other occasions, and has a couple of very fine Clint Eastwood one-liners near the beginning. After I had listened to those, however, I did not think I could face the fighting that would happen later, so I looked for something else to do. I found some hotel notepaper and wrote out a ten-page summary of what had happened, while it was still as fresh as possible in my mind, in case I needed to make a statement.

At about two in the morning, there was a knock at the door. I looked through the spy-hole and asked who was there, and an English voice replied that they were from the Consul's staff. I let them in, and was very reassured by the presence of a couple of substantial fellow-countrymen. They listened to a brief summary of what I had been through, made a note of the banal practical details that my passport and luggage were still on the plane, and said they would be around if I needed help.

After they had gone, the phone started ringing. The hotel switchboard was being very co-operative with the world's press – if any journalist rang up and asked to speak to someone who was on the plane, they were immediately put through to Mr Thexton in room 215. Ed told me the next day that he had taken a couple of calls and then put the phone under his mattress, but I was delighted to talk. America – between nine and twelve hours behind Karachi – was waking up to the hijack's end, and the calls were coming through in succession from newspaper journalists and radio stations. I was interviewed live in New York, and repeated my story across the States.

*****

Mysterious bullet-marks in the cockpit window, as seen the following day

The view from the starboard wing, looking back at R4 with the chute down – hand luggage is strewn across the wing

Looking the other way

Someone else's blood

Shrapnel scars – Row 47 is in the rear cabin, F and G are on the starboard side aft of Door R4

Bullet damage in one of the toilets

Grenade damage in the seats

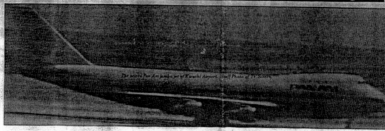

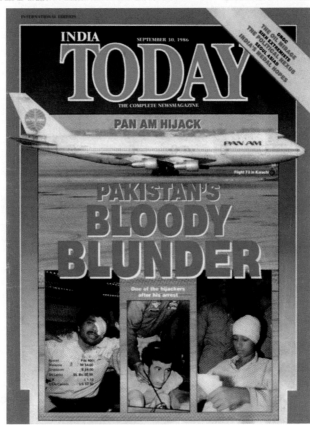

Two nations, two stories

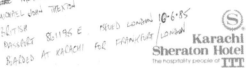

MICHAEL JOHN THEXTON
BRITISH
PASSPORT 861195 E ISSUED LONDON 10·6·85
BOARDED AT KARACHI FOR FRANKFURT/LONDON

Karachi Sheraton Hotel
The hospitality people of ITT

P O BOX 3918
CLUB ROAD KARACHI-4
TELEPHONE 521021
TELEX 25255 ASHER P.K

Last night I dozed with the light on because I didn't trust the hotel to make my early morning call at 3.15. True enough, they forgot, but I was up and ready to go by the complimentary bus to the airport just down the road. There were the normal problems — fighting off porters wanting to wheel your trolley a few paces, going through x-ray, waiting while an official first sent for a sniffer dog for my luggage and then cancelled it. At last I was through to the check-in: Clipper Class on Pan Am 073 to Frankfurt, with a connecting flight to London. I was thinking of the pleasant surprise for my parents and girlfriend when I turned up 4 days early, and how lucky I'd been to get this ticket after scouring all the airline offices — in Rawalpindi yesterday morning ....

I checked in my carefully weighed out 31 kg of luggage, just over the allowance, and tried to appear unburdened by the 14 kg of film and camera gear in my "hand luggage". These are the delig of travelling in a climbing expedition — every extra kilo precious. There were no objections at the hand search, and the unusual pleasure of the First Class lounge (a bit under in my climbing jacket, expedition tee shirt and worn-out boot o'clock and all's well — an hour or so to wait, passed d tea and reading Time magazine (practically my first news I left England 8 weeks ago). The other passengers read an about, growing more restless as 5.20 passed, then 5.45. At

The start of the statement I wrote out in the Karachi Sheraton, 5/6 September 1986

Being interviewed in the check-in area before the reserve flight brought us home

"I had you down for economy"

Taking the wounded away

Television reports

Unclaimed shoes

Someone finds hers

Trevor McDonald reads
the news

Picture from ITN archive

General Zia's press
conference

"The punishment of
which is death
sentence"

My "bloodstained hat" makes a distinctive arrival at Heathrow in the press crush

Breakfast time with Nick Ross

Frank Bough grills the Pakistani Ambassador

One of the many things that I have only understood years later: I was probably happier to talk than many people (then, and also now) because I had missed most of the gore. At this point, I did not know how many were dead and injured; I had hardly been touched. I still didn't even know about Rajesh Kumar. I had left the plane very quickly at the end, by a route that hardly anyone else used, and had hidden in a cupboard while most of the dead and injured were taken away. I was still in a state of amazed euphoria about being alive and safe when I had not expected to be. Although I came to know about the count of casualties over the next couple of days, it was less real for me than for many of those who had been on the starboard wing or who came down the chute from R4 with the injured. It probably still is less real.

*****

The last call came in at about 6 o'clock in the morning, by which time I had had no sleep at all. It was an Irish journalist trying to trace an Irishman called Sexton that he believed had been on the plane. He was disappointed that I was not Irish, but asked if he could ring back in 15 minutes and interview me anyway. I was happy to oblige, but the call never came. After a while I got hungry and decided to look for some breakfast.

The morning after

Breakfast was like a dream, for so many reasons. Even without the hijack, the sight of so much good food of so many varieties, unseen for two months, would probably have been enough to make me cry. The fact that I was still alive when I had not expected to be, added to not sleeping and feeling a little disoriented as a result, produced a strange quasi-religious state of ecstasy. I can remember looking at very mundane things – a staircase, an ashtray – and thinking how beautiful they were. People must have wondered about the rough-looking hippy in the lobby of the luxury hotel, staring in stoned amazement at interior decorations and mouthing "Wow!"

At breakfast, I met Dennis and Ed – still without shoes, but washed up a little – and we sat and talked over a few details. A copy of *The Muslim* newspaper told us that "a daring commando raid had freed the hijacked passengers". At the time, this seemed mildly amusing – we joked that there must have been another hijack going on somewhere, and we wondered where it was. We all agreed that there had been no commando raid. Dennis said that he had met a cordon of soldiers out in the darkness – he had taken the opposite direction to me, and had run away from the buildings – but none of us had seen any soldiers near the plane until after it was all over.

The story came from the first press conference given by the Pakistani authorities after the end of the hijack. It has never been clear to me whether they thought this was what had actually happened – after all, it was all quite confusing – or whether they thought it was a good story and that was what they wanted people to believe. A few hours later, they realised that it had not happened and that they could not make people believe it – there were too many survivors who would contradict it. They may also have counted the casualties and decided that it was not that great a story anyway. So a further press conference retracted it and told what had actually happened.

By that time, no-one was listening. As a proverb – one that surprisingly seems to be older than radio and television – puts it, "A lie can be halfway around the world, before the truth has gotten its trousers on". The first story had gone round the world, and history records that this hijacking ended with a storming. Whenever there is a terrorist atrocity involving a plane, journalists go to some database and trot out a calendar of past events, and it will include "September 1986, Karachi, 21 dead, ended with storming by Pakistani commandos" (the 21st casualty appears also to be a misunderstanding – the initial published list included someone called Gorgi Gopal, who does not seem to have existed).

Recently I saw such a catalogue which, at first sight, excluded "our" hijack altogether – until I realised that the location had shifted to Frankfurt (and the commandos had become anonymous – even the most careless journalist might have wondered what the Pakistanis were doing storming a Pan Am plane in Germany). I suppose the database says that the plane was on its way to Frankfurt, and someone has picked up the wrong end of the journey.

Does any of this matter? To most people, it is an unimportant little detail of history. Its main real significance is that the gang used this false story as a defence at their trial. They claimed that they did not shoot anyone: the Pakistani commandos had stormed the plane and their gunfire killed the passengers. This is a complete travesty and it does seem to have been ignored by the court, but lies make for propaganda. It could be represented to other terrorist recruits that this bunch had been unfairly convicted for something they did not do, so – let's hijack a plane to set them free, in the interests of justice! And so it goes on.

So, for the avoidance of doubt, there were no commandos. They were, quite properly, practising on a different aircraft elsewhere in the airport. There was a deadline set by the terrorists for a couple of hours later and it seems that they were going to storm the plane as that deadline drew near. The shooting started when no-one expected it, before the commandos were ready or in place. When the word reached them, they all piled into their trucks and headed for our plane. Dennis, held by the security cordon on the runway, saw them arrive and enter the plane, 15 minutes after everyone else had gone (at least, those who could leave).

I was, and am, very glad of their lateness. It would be nice if the commandos could spring into the plane and neatly "take out" the four hijackers, so rescuing the passengers. At the first shooting, people opened the doors and tried to escape. If three hundred fleeing passengers had met the commandos coming the other way, it would have been a mess. When Egyptair flight 648 was hijacked in November 1985, the storming resulted in the death of nearly all the hostages – the gunfire and the commandos' explosives set fire to the plane, and hardly anyone escaped (it seems that the commandos shot people trying to get out in case they were terrorists). The terrorist leader shot five people at point blank range while trying to force the authorities to refuel the plane, just as Abbas shot Kumar: three of those five survived. In the battle at the end, another 56 people died.

The Indians and Pakistanis on the plane had probably thought, recognising the terrorists as Arabs, that "the westerners are in front of us" – just as I had thought that the Americans would be in front of me. They would have been frightened, of course, but many of them would have believed that they were not the main targets, not directly in the line of fire. Because they were the majority of the passengers, they were the majority of the victims of the indiscriminate murder. Two Americans, both of Indian origin; three Pakistanis, including the ground crewman Kharas; two Mexicans; thirteen Indians. The oldest victim, Rajesh Kumar's 81-year old grandmother; the youngest, a 7-year old boy.

*****

The lie about the storming was already all the way round the world before we had got up. We did our best to get the truth's trousers on over breakfast, without any success in changing the historical record. The three of us must have looked quite a sight around the buffet – I was still in my expedition tee-shirt, which was very grubby (even if most of the dirt that could be washed out had been extracted) and full of holes, and Dennis and Ed did not look quite as businesslike as they normally would, Ed still having no shoes. So we were amused when someone asked us, very politely, if we had been on the hijacked plane. This was a man with a magnificent handlebar moustache and a safari suit who introduced himself as the Pakistan correspondent of the London *Times*, looking as much a part of a Graham Greene novel as the Consul had. So we told him what had really happened, and presumably his report was duly filed. I had the impression later that the resident Pakistan correspondent was perhaps not the hottest reporter – the journalists who arrived later in the day seemed to be dressed more sharply and were pushier, but no more successful in reporting the facts.

Of course, there are different ways of looking at the truth: the Indian press, and the Indian Prime Minister Rajiv Ghandi, used the outcome as something to berate the Pakistani authorities with. The front cover of *India Today* carried the headline "Pakistan's bloody blunder", making it quite clear where they thought the blame should lie.

After breakfast, I wandered around the hotel lobby talking to some of the other survivors. I was approached by some Americans who told me they were a television crew and they had arranged for some time in a Karachi studio to do an interview. They had heard from some of the others about my story, and would I mind...? So I caught a taxi with them and with the American passenger who had opened the R3 door.

I had never been in a TV studio before (I suppose most people haven't). We sat side by side in front of a camera and talked to a disembodied voice somewhere in the USA, trying to imagine that the camera itself was a face. This interview was taken by the BBC as well (although they left out the American, presumably because only a British story would be interesting enough – you can just see the edge of him sitting beside me on the recording my family made). Watching the news, my parents had a double shock – first, what I looked like (I don't think Peter had ever ended up quite so wrecked after an expedition), and second, the briefest summary of what had happened to me.

By late afternoon, I was resting in my room – perhaps finally running out of adrenalin and managing to sleep – when the telephone rang. It was one of the Consul's officers in the hotel lobby. He had my passport and asked if "a green bag that weighs a ton" might be mine. Having brought it all the way from the airport, he was kind enough to carry it up to my room. He told me that there was a pile of other stuff at the airport waiting to be collected. This directly contradicted what we had been told earlier by a Pan Am official (that nothing would be available until Sunday at the earliest), but it seemed that the facts could change rapidly, so I took a taxi to see if I could find my cameras.

Outside the terminal, I was challenged by Pakistani soldiers with rifles. I suppose I might have said, "Where were you yesterday?", but I simply told them that I had been on the hijacked plane, and they let me through. I think I must have been one of the first passengers to come to claim belongings (not least because mine were still there). The most striking thing about the area set aside for the hijack was a long, long line of shoes. So many people must have taken their footwear off and left them behind at the end. Some would not be coming back to claim them.

I walked up to the front, where an airport official was attending a check-in desk on, behind and around which a number of items were stacked. I spotted my Panama hat immediately and claimed it, then my still camera and both the cine-cameras, still in their pouches, but one missing its battery pack. The only other thing that was gone was my Sony Walkman, which had been taken out of the holster and put aside at the same time as the still camera. I suspect that someone decided it was too attractive to give back, or else the first passenger to arrive had taken a fancy to it. Pan Am later bought me a new one.

The journey home

The next morning, there seemed to be little information available about what was supposed to happen. Sometime after breakfast, a rumour passed around that Pan Am had sent a plane to take us home, and quite a large group of people gathered at the front of the hotel in the expectation – or hope – of going to the airport. I for one did not bother with checking out – I presumed that Ed was right, and Pan Am would simply pick up whatever the bill happened to be. Ed and Dennis were among the waiting crowd.

I had less luggage this time, but I still had the green bag, two cine-cameras and the holster on my waist. A bus arrived and we got onto it, still with no official announcement of what was supposed to happen. For once, the rumours were right, and we arrived at the terminal once again.

Quite a few other people had obviously got the message, because the check-in area was full of long files of people. There were probably five or six queues, and at the side of them, still a separate line of unclaimed shoes. Of course, many of the passengers had no documents at all – no tickets, no passports. We stood in line while the agents tried to identify people and find a place for them.

I don't suppose that anyone in Karachi decided that today would be a good day to blag a trip to New York, but it would probably have been possible.

The world's press had now arrived in force. On Saturday, the American TV journalists had to borrow the local station's equipment and there was only the local correspondent of *The Times*. Now there were half-a-dozen TV crews and any number of newspaper reporters going up and down the lines doing interviews, and by-and-by most of them came past me. It was a good thing that we had about three hours to kill. Once again, my parents recorded some of the clips from the BBC news – some interviews with me, and some where I am visible in the background, talking to someone else.

I talked to everyone, but was particularly pleased to meet the British journalists. I think they were particularly pleased to find that one of the most dramatic stories related to a Brit. The reporter from *The Daily Telegraph* came by with a photographer, and he took a full account and a picture.

At last, I reached the front of the line and went through the process of identification. I, for one, had my passport, so it was not so difficult for me. I was given another business class boarding pass and headed off to passport control and security.

Just after passport control, I – along with other passengers – was approached by a Pakistani policeman and asked to follow him into a small office. We were all very nervous, very jumpy, and I wondered what was going to happen now. The policeman asked me to make a statement about the hijacking. I was amazed: they had had the whole of the previous day, before the passengers had had a chance to embellish their stories talking to each other and to journalists, and we had not seen the police at all. Now, when we were just about to catch the plane and were in a very edgy state, they wanted statements. On the other hand, I was not going to make any fuss. I explained that I had written out an account in the hotel and if they had a photocopier, they could have a copy of it. They said that they had no copier and they would take the original. I said they could not have it, and asked for a pen and some paper.

I had just finished writing a one-page summary of this story (I was more succinct in those days) when an American stepped into the room, looked around, said "What is all this s***?" and simply left. I decided that he had a point – it was not sensitive victim-handling. So I signed the piece of paper and followed him. It was all I ever heard from the Pakistani authorities – they never asked me to come for the trial, or to make any further statement. I suppose they had plenty of other evidence, and a great deal of the burden fell on the flight attendants.

Someone explained that we needed to identify our hold luggage. There were two explanations doing the rounds of the passengers – one was that they didn't want to take the bags of the dead and wounded to New York, which was quite reasonable; the other was that they were worried that there might be a bomb in the hold. Our communal paranoia fed on the second idea.

We were driven past a Pan Am jumbo sitting just where the *Clipper Empress of the Seas* had been. It could have been the same plane. The bus took us on to a hangar some distance further from the terminal, where there was a pile of suitcases and other assorted luggage awaiting identification, and a truck in which the verified bags had been placed. I searched through the first pile and found one of the black plastic sausages, but could not locate the other. Eventually, I noticed it in the truck, which did nothing for my confidence about the authorities' ability to prevent a bomb getting on board. I can't believe anyone else would have claimed my bag by mistake.

When we were finally cleared to board the plane, the bus took us back out to it, and I made my way towards the front steps. The man from *The Daily Telegraph* was out by the plane with his photographer, and he called out to me: "Mr Thexton!" I turned my head, and he smiled. "I underestimated you – I had you down for economy." That explains the grin on my face in the photo his colleague took, which was definitely better than the one in the terminal building, and that was the one that appeared in the paper.

On this flight, I was still in business class, but now in the upstairs cabin behind the cockpit. The flight engineer from our plane sat next to me, and told me a few details about the start of the hijack itself. The flight attendant – American – found out who I was and made much of me. She told me that she had talked to the cabin crew, and passed on their view that my Muslim prayers had saved my life.

We were still very nervous, and the crew did their best to keep everyone calm and happy. The first announcement told us that there were doctors on board to help if anyone had any injuries, and if we needed anything at all, we only had to ask. I heard that just after take-off, one poor man in the first class cabin laid back in his reclining seat and closed his eyes, probably exhausted with the emotion of it all, and three medics pounced on him to try to revive him. They may well have *needed* to revive him after that.

I was disgusted to discover that the alcoholic beverages would be free for everyone on this flight. I mean, I had *paid* for free drink. What was worse, I knew that there would be a hundred journalists waiting at Heathrow, and I would be incoherent after more than one, so I restricted myself to a solitary gin-and-tonic in the whole journey. Life can be so unfair.

I spent a lot of the flight trying to remember whether "You Can't Beat The Experience" was Pan Am's advertising slogan, or some other airline's. I thought it would be a good one-liner to give to the journalists, but it would only work if it really belonged to Pan Am (which, in fact, it did). In the end, I couldn't remember, and I thought it would be in bad taste to check with the crew (it would actually have been in appallingly bad taste to say it to the press – I still hadn't properly absorbed how awful the hijack had been for everyone else – so maybe it's just as well that I didn't).

The pilot told us that he was taking a southerly route, possibly to make sure that we did not go through the airspace of anyone who could increase our anxieties. I believe that we went across Saudi Arabia and then north over Ethiopia and Egypt, going around the more troubled parts of the Middle East. I looked down through cloudless skies onto burned brown earth and thought about the expedition, about Pete, about my family, about going home.

The plane landed in Frankfurt at four o'clock in the afternoon, German time, although it was already quite late in the evening for us. Just over 20 passengers disembarked. We were escorted by German policemen towards a special transit lounge. We had a glimpse of what was waiting for us at Heathrow – there appeared to be only a handful of Germans on board and we saw them pass out of the secure area to face a wall of flashing cameras.

For us, the Germans had laid on a splendid tea – lots of sticky pastries. I don't think we did justice to it. I was doing my best (being a polite guest) when a white-haired American in a suit with four substantial minders entered the room. He announced "I'm from the American State Department and I want to talk to Mr Thexton". I introduced myself, still clutching a doughnut, and gave another brief summary of my story.

There was an announcement that our plane was going to leave for London, and I said that I was sorry but I had to go. One of his strong-arm men offered to carry my bag out to the plane, and I was very amused at the expression on his face when he tried to lift it. He wanted to hear the last few details as we went along.

I realised that I had not spoken to my family since Friday night. I expected that they probably would be told when I was arriving, but I asked if a message could be sent to find out if they could meet me at the airport. It seems a bit silly, looking back, to think that they might have failed to be there.

My ticket was from Islamabad to London, but I had no reservation from Frankfurt. In the summer of 1985, I had come home from Hong Kong without a reservation for the leg from Delhi to Heathrow, and had met a man in Delhi airport who had been there for three days waiting for a space on a plane. That greatly increased my negotiating skills, and I managed to get out in about ten hours. I saw him still sitting there as I went towards passport control. When I bought my Pan Am ticket, I had not expected that I would meet the same problems in Frankfurt on the way home from Karachi. Neither had I expected a special plane to be laid on for me and my fellow Brits, but circumstances had changed. We were the only people on a 737, and so we could spread ourselves out as much as we liked. I still kept off the alcohol.

Seeing the lights of London from the air is something that I always find moving, and it was very much so on this occasion. Even more of a cliché, however, was the fact that the first time I really felt *safe* – that nothing further could go wrong – was when I saw a British policeman on the ground. He was probably completely unaware of the psychological impact of his blue uniform and funny-shaped helmet, and he didn't look particularly pleased to see me (although he was surely on double-pay on a Sunday evening).

An official told us that we would not go through the normal arrivals area, and a separate room had been provided for us to meet with family and friends. There was a fairly cursory customs check, but they still asked us if we had anything to declare. Between customs and the meeting room, the TV cameras and microphones were everywhere. Someone asked me, "Is that blood on your hat?" Well, yes it was, but it's a spot smaller than a penny. Never mind! "*Mike Thexton, wearing a bloodstained hat...*" is what appeared in the next day's papers.

We were ushered into the room, and I looked around to see my parents, my girlfriend Louise, my sister Vicky, my old friend Jane, my business colleague Navzar, my old student Majid (this was becoming rather surreal – I had no idea what they were doing there). There were hugs and tears. Vicky and I looked at each other in amazement, wondering which of us was thinner. The others probably thought we might break each other.

One of the journalists managed to infiltrate the room. Louise recognised him – one of the disadvantages of being a TV presenter – and, as he tried to accost me to persuade me to go on his station's breakfast show the next morning, she floored him with a right hook. I regret having missed this, as it would have made my day – she was not normally given to violence, and was considerably smaller than him. A polite telephone call from the BBC later was the better approach, and that was the programme I appeared on.

After a short time, we all went outside and the press pressed around us again. All my family were being interviewed separately, and I could not even see them, although Louise kept a hold of my arm. Suddenly I had had enough: I said, "Where's the car, can we go home please?" A policeman directed us one way, but it turned out to be wrong, and we pushed this way and that with the gaggle following. Finally, we were in the car; we closed the doors; we went home. It was probably about eight o'clock in England, but it had been a long day for all of us.

On the news

General Zia had been at a non-aligned countries summit in Harare, Zimbabwe on 5 September. He returned to give a press conference in which he said he had challenged Colonel Gadaffy about the hijackers: "He told me that he had never heard of this group. If it exists, it is against him". He also responded strongly to suggestions that the hijackers should be extradited to America to be tried: "These hijackers have committed a crime on the soil of Pakistan, and we will try them here and we will see, according to the justice, they are... they receive... I should not say something and then tomorrow you will say he said so and they have been hanged [*a nice recognition of the fact that he was not an absolute dictator*], but I hope the courts will take full note of this and they will receive the punishment that such a crime deserves, according to the law, which the Parliament passed which deals with terrorist attacks. We have a very effective law, the punishment of which is death sentence."

I have a video of some of the newscasts of Sunday September 7. Apart from Zia's press conference, there are interviews with a number of the survivors and film of the scenes in the check-in area at Karachi. The line of unclaimed shoes is one striking image.

One survivor says that the shooting started after "they had thrown smoke grenades". Maybe he had believed the story about the commandos, but there were no smoke grenades. After all, it was completely dark, so there was no point. There were only explosives.

The most striking thing of all, though, is that the BBC newsreaders in 1986 sound so slow and so posh. They are, to my daughter's surprise, in colour, and wearing clothes rather than animal skins, but it seems almost like the fifties rather than the eighties. I suppose it is a lifetime ago.

Breakfast Time

On the Monday morning, I was to be on BBC Breakfast Time just after the eight o'clock news, so a car came to pick Louise and me up at about seven. BBC Television Centre is only a short drive from where I lived, so there was plenty of time for the things I had no idea about – being made up, being briefed about where I would sit and who would speak to me, waiting in the green room.

I suppose that there is always a strange mixture of people on most days on breakfast television. When I went into the green room, the famous photographer Norman Parkinson was chatting to the pop group the Pet Shop Boys. I'm not sure whether they had already been "done" or were waiting to go on after me, but I just sat in the corner with Louise and watched the start of the eight o'clock news. Then I was called and went to sit on a comfortable chair next to Nick Ross, a few yards from Frank Bough – faces so familiar to me that it was extraordinary to see them in the flesh.

Back in the green room, Louise told Norman Parkinson and the Pet Shop Boys to shut up so she could hear the interview. She must have looked like the sort of woman who could knock down a reporter with a single punch, because they did.

I've put the whole of the interview at the back of the book, because I think the way a journalist asks questions is interesting. Most of it invited me to relate the main events of the hijack, so I won't repeat it here. Nick Ross's closing remark is worth a comment:

"Well, Mike, we all delighted and relieved that you got back, not just in such good physical shape, but so well psychologically as well. Thank you very much for retelling your experiences. And I hope that in a way it's cathartic and helps to tell the story rather than dredging it all up again."

Nick Ross was (and is) a good, sympathetic interviewer, and I have no doubt that he was sincere in his suggestion that talking about the traumatic event helps the victim to deal with it. I am sure that is true, but talking about it to journalists is quite different from talking to a proper counsellor. There need be no harm in either of the two, but I don't think anyone should confuse them. The journalist is not there to help – he or she wants readers, wants viewers. The general conversation with journalists – which I was now quite familiar with – went: "How did it begin?", and then, "Tell me about getting singled out", and then, "And how did it end?" I would dutifully answer the questions, and that would be that. But I kept thinking afterwards, *that wasn't it at all*. That was the excitement, the action. But what it was *like* – the fear, the tedium, the physical discomfort, the hours of conviction that I was going to die – they hadn't touched that at all. Nor can they: news journalists haven't time or space to cover all that. Feature writers probably could, but they come later.

I wasn't as badly damaged by the journalists' attentions as the people who get a microphone shoved in their face and asked, "How do you feel about your husband being murdered?", but I understand the effect on them (without having to ask them to describe it). The journalists have a job to do, and if they can do it with reasonable sensitivity, fair enough. But I don't think journalists should ever fool themselves that they are helping the victim to deal with trauma. It may happen occasionally by accident, but it's dishonest to think it's a routine benefit of news reporting.

*****

Back in the green room, Norman and the Boys shook my hand and congratulated me warmly on my survival. Frank Bough was grilling the Pakistani ambassador, Ali Arshad. Mike Thexton has left the building...

The famous quotation is that "an ambassador is an honest man sent to lie abroad for the good of his country": he was doing his best that morning to respond to the claims of bungling and incompetence that appeared in the British and Indian press. Some of the things he said were true, others were perhaps not the whole truth, and some were slightly less than the truth. I think this version of events is illuminating, so here is the whole interview.

FB   Well, the ordeal for the victims of the Karachi hijack may be over, but questions surrounding the tragic end are still being asked. General Zia of Pakistan has rejected the criticisms of his country's handling of the hijack and has insisted that the four hijackers will be tried in Pakistan, where such a crime carries the death penalty. With me now is Pakistan's Ambassador to London, Mr Ali Arshad. A very good morning to you. There have been criticisms, largely that it was twenty-five minutes before your special guys, actually from the time the first shots were fired to when they actually got on the plane.

AA   I've been in touch with the authorities concerned, and this story is entirely wrong.

FB   It's not a story, it's admitted by the man who's the boss of the FAS, Brigadier ....

AA   No, he's alleged to have said it, but he hasn't said it. I spoke to the Secretary of Defence, who's in charge of this operation, from the other end in Islamabad, and he told me that he had personally interviewed the leader of the commandos, who told him that it took them exactly three minutes to reach the plane and to take it. Actually the indiscriminate shooting had finally made them go into action. They were reacting to the situation. There was no previous plan to storm the plane at any particular moment. There had been various plans beforehand, various scenarios, and they were actually ready to go into action. The action they went into was a reaction to that indiscriminate...

FB   Well, where have all these stories come from, because they have a tremendous amount of backing from very authoritative people, that the people who were going to attack the plane, should it be necessary, were in fact familiarising themselves with the interior of another 747, rather a long way on the other side of the airport? So it must have taken them quite a long time to get to the …

AA   No, well Karachi airport is not a very large airport, and it should not be very difficult to reach a plane from a distance of about 300 yards or so. The commandos were already there at 1.30 in the afternoon. It's true that they were taken to this other plane so that they may see the layout of the plane and to familiarise themselves with the layout. And that was the reason why they were taken there, so that they might be able to plan their action, when the need arose.

FB   Now are there not lessons to be learned, because it's unquestionable, isn't it, that they actually got onto the airport very easily – they drove in without passes, so presumably you are looking very closely at your security measures?

AA   It is not very clear how exactly they gained access. According to one of the stories, they stormed their way through the cargo entrance. Investigations are going on and we'll know the detail later on.

FB   So you have all four of them in custody.

AA   We have all four of them in custody, one of them is seriously injured, the other three have minor injuries.

FB   And they will be tried when?

AA   They will be tried in the near future, and when convicted, they will be properly dealt with according to the law of the land, which is very very strict on this issue.

FB   I wonder if the authorities in Pakistan have thought about possible retaliation, has that played any part in your…?

AA   Retaliation from what direction?

FB   Well, you've now got the four men, somebody presumably might want them out, or if you hang them as you may well do, or execute them, there may be retaliation, have you thought of that?

AA   Well, nevertheless, the law of the land has to take its course, and we shall go ahead with the trial. The recent statement etcetera in the press, and allegations in the press, in *The Sunday Times*, saying that it was the blunders of the Pakistanis that led to the massacre, they are entirely wrong. They seem to allege that there were certain warnings given to the government of Pakistan. There were absolutely no warnings, and if there were any, why don't the governments which warned us come forward and say that we have done this? There were no warnings, there was no high alert. It was just the normal alert which is at an airport. They came dressed as security guards, and that sort of thing can happen almost anywhere. And if it is only a question of passes, if they could get everything else they could have also obtained passes.

FB   Ambassador, we must stop there, thank you...

Three minutes to get to the plane, starting when? It may have been three minutes from the moment that the commandos were told that they were needed, but I prefer to believe Dennis's statement that they arrived fifteen minutes after the shooting stopped. I don't think that's their fault, and as I have said, I am glad that I had the opportunity to get out before they were coming the other way; it seems to me that the ambassador was trying to bat away an unreasonable criticism with an untrue defence.

I'm not sure that government intelligence services freely announce on a regular basis that they have been giving warnings, either – the absence of a CIA spokesperson saying "We told you so" is not evidence that they didn't. They may have, they may not: rumours of warnings are inevitable after any such incident.

At lunchtime on Monday, I went to Hyde Park Corner to the studios of an American station, to be on breakfast time in the USA as well. I was collected from home by a cheerful driver who asked me if I had enjoyed the "gang bang" at Heathrow – the gentlemen of the press have a way with words.

A British teenager (with an Indian or Pakistani name – perhaps his passport was safer than mine) was already there, and we sat side by side to talk to the cameras. We were told we had to wait for the buses – five red double-deckers rolled past the window and we could proceed. The studio director said that they were always laid on for interviews from London, so the Americans would know where they were looking at. They probably say that to all the gullible interviewees sitting in their studio for the first time.

I can remember the interviewer from America asking, "Did you think of jumping them?" and the lad and I looked at each other with an almost telepathic understanding that said, "These guys! Shall I tell him or do you want to?"

I looked at all the press coverage. I was appalled by the treatment handed to the flight crew, and I wrote a letter to one paper defending their actions – it was published, but probably changed no-one's opinion. On the other hand, I was amused by what I am sure was a misprint in *The Guardian*, which is famous for them: a Department of Transport official was quoted as saying, "It could happen here". I am sure he said that it could *not* happen here – indeed, I would be very surprised if anyone could pull off a similar stunt at a British airport, then or now, and I would expect a much better response by the authorities, in the negotiation, the security cordon, the storming, the medical facilities, and the general organisation. If the civil servant really thought it could happen here, he was being surprisingly frank. These were the days before spin, I suppose.

*****

On the Tuesday, I went back to Heathrow to meet the returning climbers, who I had said goodbye to a lifetime before on the previous Thursday. I didn't know whether they had any idea about what had happened to me. They had seen the news on the Friday and had put it together: after all, one of the others had been in the Pan Am office with me. They spent the day in the British Embassy club listening to the news and worrying. We went to a pub so I could tell them the tale. They sat and listened in amazement that the expedition wimp could have survived such a thing, and could have jumped off the wing of a jumbo jet.

I never asked them how they got the petechiometers home.

Of course, Tuesday was supposed to be the day I went back to work – that was my excuse for rearranging my flight in the first place. In all the circumstances, I decided to have a few more days off.

On the Wednesday, a man came from the American Embassy to interview me, in the company of a British policeman from the anti-terrorist squad. On Thursday, I went up to Whitehall to be debriefed by the British authorities at the Foreign Office. This interview was quite different from talking to journalists. Here were people who wanted to know everything about everything, the tedious details as well as the exciting action, and I believe that this really did act as counselling for me. It was not intended to, but it enabled me to speak about every aspect of the experience to people with a professional interest, and I am sure that was a good thing.

There were people from the Foreign Office itself; Ministry of Defence; Metropolitan Police; Department of Transport; probably others. There was also another passenger who I had not previously met, an executive from an international corporation. Because he worked for a big company which had strong links with government, his employer offered his assistance to the authorities. We talked through our separate experiences from start to finish, and it took the whole morning.

I remember the man from the Ministry of Defence asking me to identify the guns I had seen. He had a book with pictures in, and showed me a page of rifles. I was rather disappointed to say that none of them resembled what I remembered. He turned to another page, and I said, "That's it!" immediately. "I thought so, a Kalashnikov." I suppose he showed me the other page first to see if I would just point to the first gun. I could not identify the handguns or grenades, though.

Afterwards, they took us to lunch in a pub. On finding out that I was an accountant, one of the officials said that I must have looked at all the debits and credits in my life and weighed them up – were the debits bigger, or the credits? "They were exactly equal, of course", I replied, which I was quite proud of. Oscar Wilde might have appreciated it, if only he had ever drawn up a trial balance.

One of the others approached us after lunch. "Gentlemen, that was magnificent." He looked a little sheepish. "This may be a bit of a liberty, and please feel free to say no, but I run the hostage negotiators course at Hendon Police College for the Metropolitan Police, and I have a course running next week and it would be fantastic if you could come and tell us the story again." The other man and I looked at each other and agreed immediately. We have been doing it four times a year ever since.

My last television exposure that week was recording the Sunday morning "thought for the day" for TV-AM. They asked my father for his thoughts as a minister of religion, and he suggested that my thoughts might be more interesting and relevant. So I wrote something up and went to their studios in Camden Town, and had my first and only experience of reading an autocue.

Recently there has been a debate about whether people who read autocues are worth the money. The producer insisted that I must have done it before, because I was ad libbing as I went along, improving (I hoped) the flow of the text. It did seem just like reading aloud to me – sadly, they did not immediately offer me a job presenting the news. I've put the result in the appendices at the back of the book – by this stage, you will appreciate that I was being asked to tell the story again and again, and you will probably also appreciate me not telling it again to you.

What the papers say

There is a saying – that I can't trace – that "every story in a newspaper is absolutely true except for the one of which you have personal knowledge, which is completely false". Looking at my cuttings from September 1986, that is perhaps a little unfair, but there are certainly some inaccuracies. The big one – that there was a storming – was already being corrected by the papers on Monday morning, but the proverb about the truth and its trousers was borne out. Some of the stories continued to report a storming, and a little Googling today will show that most of them still do.

The Guardian reported: "*Mr Mike Thexton, a medical student on his way back from a climbing expedition...*" and, quoting my description of the end, *"the guy next to me wanted to stay put but I pushed him to one side and jumped on the wing"*. At least they printed my letter later in the week: "*I was surprised to find myself to be a medical student in your hi-jack report of September 8: I am an accountancy lecturer. And I was upset to be quoted as saying that I pushed another passenger to one side in my efforts to get out. Although I was too frightened to be one of the heroes, I was not trampling on the other people to save myself. What I actually said was, 'I pushed him out in front of me', for which he thanked me later.*"

The Daily Mail reported the views of a wounded 16-year old who criticised the pilot for escaping: "*He could have calmed the people, and they wouldn't have started shooting finally, and wouldn't have got me. He could have told them, 'Let the women and children go and I will fly you wherever you want to go'.*" This is related beneath a picture of Captain William Kianka, 52, home safe in Hopewell, New Jersey, with his wife and his own 16-year old daughter. He is quoted as saying that he had no regrets about leaving the plane. "*What we did was my own decision. I don't care what anyone thinks – one just has to look at the amount of survivors who came through this.*" There is no editorial comment, but the headline is "*Air hijack girl blames captain who left plane*".

I think the 6 September 1986 report from *The Muslim*, the Pakistani newspaper, is also worth quoting at some length. Hindsight is, of course, a wonderful thing; the morning after the confusing events of the day before, there were a lot of things that were not straightened out. Here are some extracts. There were a few accurate comments, but the newspaper (and, if he is accurately quoted) the Air Marshal were very specific about things that didn't happen.

"Fifteen people were killed [actually 20] *and 65 injured* [at least a hundred] *during the operation* [what operation?] *to free the hijacked American Jumbo jet at Karachi airport tonight. Among the dead two were hijackers* [all four survived].

The injuries were caused when the passengers escaped through emergency exits... [some were caused by jumping off wings, but the worst were caused before the doors were open].

The PTV bulletin said the hijackers fired on the commandos during the operation [the hijackers had run out of ammunition before the commandos arrived] *and the front of the plane blew up after an explosion* [the photographs show that this is an exaggeration]. *However it did not say whether the hijackers also fired at the passengers or not...* [well, they did].

In the first shootout that took place at time of the seizure of the plane an American national with Indian origin, Rajesh Kumar aged 30, was killed. He was hit in the head while escaping from the aircraft... [he was shot about three hours after the start, and if it wasn't so appallingly tragic, the idea that he was "shot while escaping" would be funny].

Giving details about the operation, he [Air Marshal Mirza] *said the tarmac lights which had been flood-lighting the aircraft and the adjacent area had been turned off before the operation began. The internal lights of the aircraft went off some time earlier after the generator on board the plane stopped functioning due to falling oil level. He added that the generator had been functioning since this morning as the engine had to be kept on to keep the air conditioning plant running, so the oil level of the generator dropped and it stopped functioning* [that might actually be true, but Mirza makes it sound as if the whole thing had been planned].

Mr Mirza said the hijackers had requested that the tarmac lights be turned on, but in the meantime army commandos, who were stationed, hiding nearby, moved in under the cover of darkness [this did not happen – they arrived in trucks after the shooting was finished].

Replying to a question, the DGCAA [Director General, Civil Aviation Authority – Mirza] *categorically said that the hijackers, who had become very edgy before the operation, had even begun shooting. The law enforcing agencies returned the fire* [I don't think so].

In the meantime, the passengers were told to leave the aircraft by emergency exits, and they did so... [told by whom?].

The DGCAA said the casualties were fairly light considering the type of operation launched to free the passengers. Less than five per cent of the passengers sustained injuries, fatal, serious or minor he added."

As the report had already given the number of people on board as 389 passengers and cabin crew (which seems to be a reasonably consistent figure in other reports as well, and may even be accurate), five per cent ought to be just under 20 people hurt. The understated report of 15 dead and 65 injured – 80 casualties out of 389 – is over 20 per cent. The actual figure – about 120 casualties – is over 30 per cent. As an accountant, these things bother me.

Through the week, the news interest declined, from the national papers to the local press. The last request came from one of the Sunday papers – they had rather missed out on interviews immediately after the hijack, because they did not have people on the ground in Karachi and the passengers only arrived home on Sunday evening. Someone rang me on Friday and asked if I would pose with Louise for a human interest piece, "doing something normal together", like shopping. At this point I decided that my 15 minutes of fame were up, and politely declined.

WHAT HAPPENED TO THE HIPPY MAN

I found later that it is possible to qualify for a little stoppage time on those 15 minutes of fame. In the period immediately after the hijack, I discovered that I was the subject of "JFK syndrome" – quite a few people told me "where I was when I heard about the hijack". One of my friends had seen me on the television while he was collecting a Chinese takeaway, and had to explain to the other customers why he got so excited.

My oldest friend was driving up to Derbyshire for the weekend with his girlfriend and a couple of other people in the car. My parents had told him what was happening, and they were listening intently to the radio for the latest developments. They had driven at great speed along the wrong side of the A52 for several miles before someone pointed out that it wasn't a dual carriageway. I would have been disappointed to find that I had survived the terrorist attack but had indirectly caused the death of my closest friends.

Because I had worked in training, giving courses to large classes of accountants, there were many people who would recognise my name, and the story became common property in the firm where I had been employed. A couple of years afterwards, a friend told me, "You wouldn't believe the innocent enjoyment your story has created. The other day someone told me – someone I didn't think knew you very well – that his close friend Mike Thexton had been hijacked by the IRA at Athens airport...".

*****

I was back on Breakfast Time in December as one of their "people of the year" – finding out that it is easy to agree to do all sorts of odd things when a TV crew suggests them, such as sitting looking thoughtful on a bench by the River Thames (I don't do that very often) or letting my mother be persuaded to be filmed doing some washing up (to be appropriately "motherly").

Although the journalists' database about stormings may be unreliable, I was on a list somewhere of people who have been hijacked, so I received requests for comments and input for newspaper stories and television programmes on hostage-taking and hijacking. In 1987, I appeared in a daytime show about the experience of being a hostage with Sheila Matthews from the Balcombe Street siege and Sir Geoffrey Jackson, who was the British Ambassador to Uruguay and was held by rebel guerrillas for eight months in 1971.

I was also one of the invited guests on a morning chat show about the Beirut hostages, just after a French hostage had been released. It seemed likely that the French government had given something for his release: I expressed the view that governments should not negotiate with hostage-takers. I did not understand then that there are different levels of negotiation – it may be possible to help a hostage without giving in, or even giving the other side the hope that you will give in, but that is a very difficult balance. I remember Jill Morrell, the girlfriend of John McCarthy – who was still in the middle of his long incarceration in Beirut – trying to make this point on the same programme, and I disagreed strongly with her. She probably knew a lot more about it than me.

In the spring of 1988, a Kuwait Air jet was hijacked in the Mediterranean, and this time the hostages were whittled down to a manageable few and flown around from country to country, ending in Tunisia. I was asked to appear on another morning chat show to discuss hijacking, and I couldn't make it. I asked my friend from the negotiators' courses, but he said he didn't want to, so I tried the number I had for Dennis. He came down to London from Stoke, and I met up with him for a drink the night before the show.

I can't say how much of dealing with trauma is to do with the character of the individual and how much is to do with the treatment. All I can say is that Dennis had not had the benefit of being debriefed by the Foreign Office or at any number of courses after that, and he was much more troubled by his memories than I was. He was "just an ordinary hostage", unlike me; and he lived in Stoke, so he was less convenient to interview. A year after I was hijacked, the Zeebrugge ferry capsized, and it was recognised after that that the survivors needed counselling. When Dennis arrived at Heathrow, he just went home to Stoke, and was left to get on with it.

He told me that he had tried telling his wife about it, but she became too distressed, and so he felt he could not share it with her. His work colleagues asked him to tell them, expecting an exciting yarn, and he gave them the bloody mess without any jokes at all. They didn't want to hear it again. It may be that he was less jumpy on normal days when he was not about to have to recall it all the next morning on live television, but he seemed to me to still be suffering badly from his experience.

As that hijack progressed, I was asked to appear on BBC Breakfast Time again. A researcher rang up to book me for the next morning's show about ten minutes after I had agreed to help out an accountancy college which had been let down by a lecturer and needed an emergency replacement in Milton Keynes that same morning. The researcher couldn't quite believe that I would turn down an appearance on the television for that, but I insisted. My word was my bond. So, a few minutes later, she rang back with a promise that the car would collect me from my home, deliver me to the studio for a short interview just after eight o'clock, and then get me to Milton Keynes by nine o'clock. And would come and collect me at the end of my day's lecturing and bring me home again.

The researcher asked me questions about whether I thought the Kuwaiti plane should be stormed. I pointed out that our plane had not been stormed, and she expressed surprise. According to her database, we had been rescued by commandos. I said that I was perfectly prepared to come on the programme and talk, as long as she was aware that I didn't have first-hand knowledge of a storming.

I was duly collected and went to the studio, complete with accountancy notes for afterwards. I was ushered into a seat next to John Stapleton while the 8 o'clock news was being read; then he spoke to camera (reading the autocue) and suggested that the situation might be resolved by storming the plane. Then he said he had someone with him who had been hijacked in 1986, and turned to me to ask what I had felt when the Pakistani commandos came aboard the plane.

"?.....?" This is the point at which the autocue gives no assistance. I think I said something like, "Well, the Pakistani commandos didn't actually storm the plane, and I think it would have been a lot more dangerous for the passengers if they had." After that, he talked across me to his other guest for the next ten minutes, before I had a chance to slope off and get my car to Milton Keynes. A great success.

There were three good things about this – one was my arrival at the college in a BBC limo at exactly 8.59, with all the students waiting outside the building wondering if they were being let down again, and then wondering just who they were getting. Then there was the student (only one) who had been watching Breakfast Time and sat staring at me curiously through the first part of the morning before I explained that yes, it had been me. Best was the postcard I received from a friend a couple of days later:

"Watched Breakfast Time this morning for the first time ever. You were on it. Are you always on it?" The power of extrapolation from a small sample (sorry, back to matters of accountancy again).

Dealing with it

People often asked me in the early days if I had nightmares. I suppose I had three or four then, and I have had three or four since, which is not bad over two decades. People who have never been hijacked probably have as many. My worst recurring nightmare, which comes in many different forms but always has the same theme, is being late for an accountancy lecture. I have forgotten where it is, or a series of problems keeps holding me up, or I have gone to the wrong place. This once happened to me on the way to a hijack lecture – I went to the Department of Transport instead of the Ministry of Defence, and arrived about forty minutes late after finding it very difficult to work out where I was actually supposed to be. And then someone asked me if I had nightmares – about being hijacked!

From the very beginning, I did not feel particularly angry with the hijackers. I think that this was the result of determining on the day that I would not die angry with them, and surprised by survival, I could not resurrect any anger afterwards. Some people think that this is the same as having sympathy for them. It is not. For some years, I believed that they should be put to death for what they had done. That was not a belief born of anger or a desire for revenge: it was the only result that I thought would represent justice. Nothing else seemed to take seriously enough the awful thing they had done.

Soon after I returned I heard that there was a British survivor, Catherine Hill, in the Central Middlesex Hospital. She had been caught in a grenade blast on the plane. I called on her to leave flowers while she slept after one of her many operations, and then visited her a couple of times while she was rehabilitating in a specialist hospital north of London. What they did to her was horrible, unforgivable – or, at least, unforgivable by me. I could forgive them for what they did to me, but not for what they did to other people.

When I saw how crippled she was, and would remain, I finally began to appreciate the horror of what had happened. She had to use a peculiar rubber cushion at all times to make sitting bearable and to avoid sores on her wounded flesh. She could just about walk, on crutches, but was obviously in pain. I did not like to ask about her prospects for recovery or the grim details of what had happened to her insides, but I could guess the main points.

For the first time, I really *knew* how lucky I was to have walked away with a scratched elbow and a few bad dreams. I felt "survivor guilt" – it really ought to have been me and not her, not Neerja, not Kharas, not a 7-year old child. It's a peculiar feeling. Fortunately, I never felt it very strongly, and I never had a serious problem with it, but it's discomforting to sit with someone who was so much unluckier. Whether Catherine was thinking it or not, I could imagine the reverse idea would occur to her. Why was I walking and free of pain when she was in a wheelchair? Why could I have a family when she could not?

I am sure that a physical injury makes the mental trauma much worse. If you are badly hurt, then you will have something to remind you of the event every day. On the great majority of days I do not think about it at all – but if I had lost a leg, or even just a finger, then the wound and the gap would always be there to keep my mind raw and painful, even after the physical hurt might have diminished.

I am sure that talking about it regularly and fully – not just the blood and excitement – was very helpful. I have probably told the story more than two hundred times to police negotiators in England, Scotland, and Seattle; commandos; army officers; army interrogation specialists (I never quite understood their interest, but to refuse might be dangerous!); civil aircrew instructors; and, very occasionally, commercial courses – one public conference run by an organisation called "Survival Aids", and once for the crisis management committee of a large company. I have spent far more of my life talking about being hijacked than actually being hijacked (I suppose that could go for a few other activities as well).

Normally, I just tell the story of the hijack itself, selecting parts that are important to the audience. The negotiators need to understand the way in which the hostage-takers may behave and may interact with the hostages, as well as needing to appreciate the needs of the hostages (who can easily become a bit of an inconvenience in a technical training exercise when the negotiator wants to use the skills from the manual). The negotiators also need to know that unexpected things can throw the whole exercise completely off its nicely planned track – smoking in the toilet! – and to take to heart the knowledge that the death of a hostage is *not their fault*. They can only do their best to sort out a mess of someone else's making; they have to be able to walk away, and be ready to do their best again another day, even if it doesn't end happily. That can't be easy.

The commandos need to know where people might be when they burst in, and how the passengers might react to shooting. I have only talked to the SAS, and have never seen them doing an exercise, but I remember one of the officers commenting to me after my talk: "They had passengers sitting in the aisles and round the doors? That would be inconvenient. When we do an exercise, we sit the hostages in the seats. Then we come in through the doors and run up and down the aisles." He said he would think about it.

It must be hard for the SAS to live with the level of public expectation. A programme called "Crisis" in the late 1980s simulated the Cabinet committee procedure for dealing with an international incident, involving a number of ex-government ministers and retired military and security people. They ended up "sending in the SAS" to end a hijack in Beirut; the programme-makers told them that ten of the commandos and several hostages had died in the raid, and they had to assess whether it had been a success or not. I was asked to provide "expert comment" in the phone-in afterwards. The thing that struck me was how people rang up to say that it was not credible: ten SAS dead, and not achieving a perfect rescue of all the hostages? That surely wouldn't happen in real life.

It's nice to think that they are endowed with super-powers, but in a darkened plane full of passengers and men firing Kalashnikovs at random, I think I'd rather they were exactly where the Pakistani commandos were – on the other side of the airport.

The aircrew instructors need to know that the passengers want the pilot off the plane as quickly as possible, and preferably carrying the tape of "The Entertainer".

Normally, I also put the jokes in and tell my story in a light-hearted manner. The first time I flew anywhere after returning from Pakistan was to give a lecture on financial services law in Guernsey in November 1986. Continuing my media saturation that year, the visit of a lecturer from the mainland made the front page of the local paper, next to – and slightly smaller than – a story about a ferret killing 43 chickens. The people who had asked me to come took me out to dinner and, having heard a rumour about my "recent adventure", asked me to tell them the story. I was feeling jumpy and frayed at the edges after a simple plane journey on a small aircraft, and I told them the story without any jokes at all. I don't think they enjoyed it. They probably wished they'd asked for a preview of my law lecture.

After many years and many tellings, I hope that the story is still as accurate as it was when I was first debriefed at the Foreign Office. For several years, I had to present it annually with the same senior police officer sitting in the front row, and I think his presence stopped me exaggerating. Most of the time, I can tell the tale as if it happened to someone else. If I stop for a moment and think, I can still put myself in the picture, and remember that this is about me; but most of the time it is just a cracking good story. That is also a way of dealing with it.

Putting something different in the telling is dangerous. On one occasion, a visiting FBI agent told me about the examination of the crime scene, and he mentioned that his men – who had to search the plane on its arrival back in Miami – had been astonished at how much blood there was in the seats. They had seen many gory sights, but this was particularly bad. The next time I told the story, I put in this detail, and nearly burst into tears. Suddenly it had become real again: that was the blood of innocent people who died, innocent people who were maimed. Only by a miracle, not my blood. A little too real.

*****

If you are injured on an aircraft, you can claim compensation within what is called the Montreal Protocol to the Warsaw Convention. The liability of the airline was restricted at that time to $20,000, but it was not necessary to prove negligence. One of my relations is a lawyer, and he encouraged me to get a psychiatric assessment to see if I might have a claim. I was fairly indifferent about this, but seeing the shrink might be interesting.

My mother put me in touch with her colleague Dr Tom Main. This was a little peculiar, as they worked together in the Institute of Psychosexual Medicine, and this was probably not my problem (well, not arising from the hijack, anyway). However, his first major work had been on the after-effects of the Second World War on soldiers – he was one of the "inventors" of post-traumatic stress syndrome. So he seemed an appropriate man to talk to.

I think I went to see him three times. He started out by telling me that he knew that his report was to justify a claim in damages, and that would be fine; I protested that I didn't feel that damaged, and he told me not to feel guilty about it and to take the money. This was an interesting start to the consultation – I hadn't been feeling that guilty, and now my shrink was telling me to stop it.

The next strange thing was that he wanted to talk about my brother rather than the hijack. He seemed to think that bereavement was a more interesting subject: "You must have been very angry with your brother when he died. He was your older brother, stronger, faster, bigger – what a betrayal for him to die."

"No, I don't think I felt angry with him. I felt sad, but mountaineering was what he did – I couldn't have asked him to not do it."

"I wonder why you are suppressing your feelings of anger with your brother...".

He went on to suggest that the suppression of the "normal" anger a bereaved person feels had probably led on to the suppression of the very healthy anger I ought to be feeling towards the hijackers. After three hours of this, I was thoroughly mixed up, and not a little angry, mainly with him. He wrote a report that made a very convincing case that I was fundamentally damaged by the hijack experience and would never recover – I assume that he was doing what he thought was right and proper to win me some compensation, but I wish he had made it a little easier for me to see that he didn't mean it. I never thought I was nuts until I went to see Dr Main.

Actually, there were several people who were willing to offer testimony to Pan Am that I was a hopeless case anyway and the hijack changed nothing, but the insurers paid up $4,000.

Of course, compensation would have been more urgent if I had really needed the money – if I had been injured. Catherine Hilll had a long fight to put her life back together, to get her complex and lengthy medical treatment paid for, and to ensure some financial security to replace the prospects she had once had.

She had little choice but to sue Pan Am: who else would pay? I find it hard to see Pan Am as anything other than victims of this with the rest of us. They could hardly have done anything about the airport security, except possibly refuse to land in most airports in the world until it was improved. The main point of contention was the departure of the flight crew; I have explained why I think that was a good thing. The break-down of the auxiliary power unit was predictable, but I don't think Pan Am could have done very much about it. It was down to the authorities by that time: they needed to have seen it coming and done more to avert the crisis.

At least there is a semi-happy ending: Pan Am's insurers did pay her in the end, after years of argument.

Heathrow before (13 July 1986) …

… and after (7 September 1986)

143

A normal day back at work – just me, a class of accountants…

…and a BBC camera crew

Struggling with the question about the storming that didn't happen, 12 April 1988

Surprised to see one of the men for whom we were hijacked in the London Evening Standard, 1 October 1993

Whodunit? Abu Nidal surely gave the order…

Ian Davison at Heathrow after his flight from Cyprus

PLO killer flies in with nowhere to go

PLO killer Ian Davison arrived back in Britain last night after being freed from a life sentence in Cyprus — and found he had nowhere to go.

Hours earlier, he had been released under an amnesty and deported from the island after serving eight years for his part in murdering three Israelis.

Davison, 35, a former carpenter from South Shields, Tyne and Wear, who said he was working for the PLO when the killings took place in

STANDARD REPORTER

1985, passed through Heathrow with the minimum of formalities but waited several hours before leaving the arrivals area.

There was no one to greet him at the airport and he made several phone calls to locate friends in the London area.

A policeman said: "We have not been questioning him. He is just trying to find somewhere to lay his head for the night."

…but who paid him?

The IRA have their go at the Thexton family, 11 April 1992

`4` THE PEOPLE, April 12, 1992

DIY supers

BLAST, IT'S OUR WEDDING DAY!

By DANNY BUCKLAND

A DEFIANT couple went ahead with their marriage yesterday despite the IRA bombers wrecking their wedding church.

Rubble filled the aisle of historic St Helen's Church in the City of London after the beautiful stained glass windows were blown in.

But doctor Vicky Thexton and surgeon Chris Lavy were determined that nothing was going to spoil their big day.

And curate Hugh Palmer was able to organise a last-minute switch to a different church.

Vicky, 27, said: "He was brilliant in fixing things up. Today's been a bit hectic, phoning all the guests about the new venue.

"But Chris and I are going to work in Zambia soon and this was the only weekend we could marry."

VICKY: Brave bride

A clutch of hostages, Army Staff College 10 September 1992

Me, without beard, Karachi Airport
5 September 1986, 16 hours

PC Trevor Lock GM, London Iranian Embassy
April/May 1980, 6 days

Terry Waite CBE, Beirut
January 1987 to November 1991, 1,760 days

With us are Major-General HM Rose CBE QGM; DAC DC Veness;
Professor P Wilkinson

"In the same boat"

Sir Geoffrey Jackson,
Uruguay, 1971, 8 months

Sheila Matthews, Balcombe
Street London, 1975, 6 days

Ali/Ismail/Jamal
as he was then…

Letter from Jamal

bute. Despite the lunacy ... dle East, we have many forums ... & accommadation. And I believe the day won't be far when we will have peace. An everlasting one.

I have a few ideas of my own. Even being hunted by the Americans will not deter or make me change. However, I hope I'll be able to devote time to the handicapped in memory of a friend who died last year. She had devoted her whole life unrelentessly to the cause of handicapped. And of course, I wish to work for peace in Palestine. Beside joining in efforts of enabling individual reconcilians on both the sides. I have to start somewhere. That is a reason why I wrote to you.

with Best Wishes

Yours

Jamal.

… and as he is now

Washington DC, May 2004

Mr and Mrs Viraf Daroga (the man with the megaphone)

The avenging angels, Gregg Maisel and Jennifer Levy

Sunshine and me

Neerja Bhanot Awards 2000

A trust was set up in Neerja's memory to honour women who show comparable courage and dedication to duty

Flight Safety Foundation Award to Neerja

NAME OF INMATE:	REGISTER NUMBER:
ZAID SAFARINI	14361-006
1. ☒ The inmate is eligible for parole as of May 31, 2038.	2. ☐ Inmate is eligible for release on parole at the discretion of the U.S. Parole Commission.
3. ☐ Inmate is on furlough From:_____ To:_____	(Destination City and State)
4. ☐ Inmate is being transferred to a community corrections center on _____ (Date). The name of the center is _____ . Located in (city and state) _____ .	
5a. ☒ Inmate's Release Date: October 4, 2108.	

Bureau of Prisons notification – the release date seems a bit early for 160 years

What happened to the hippy man? He put on weight and bought a beard trimmer – but never threw anything away

For two years after the hijack, I believe that I thought about it every day. This was not in any state of fear or horror: it was just always running through my mind. Some might say that telling the story over and over again to courses would have helped to keep it this vivid for me, but I have also been told that two years is a reasonably typical length of time for such a thing to stay with a person.

On 5 September 1988, I returned home from work to find a card from Louise. It wished me a "happy second birthday". I realised that it was "the day", and I had not thought about it at all. I must have been getting better.

*****

I had split up with Louise in 1987. In 1990 I married Kathy, an American. She has recently taken British nationality as well, so that she will not automatically be in front of me when the passports are next collected in. We have two daughters who have one passport of each type.

We live under the landing flightpath into Heathrow so I can watch the jumbo jets go by.

1992

I was probably a little paranoid before the hijack, but certainly more so afterwards. It's much more comforting to say "terrorism happens to other people" – although having been "done" once, I ought to have been much more confident that nothing could happen to me again, rather than more fearful. I would keep my eyes open in airports. I read the emergency instructions and noted whether the nearest usable exit was behind me. I wondered about bombs even in city streets.

On Friday April 10, 1992, most of my family was in St Helen's Church off Bishopsgate for the rehearsal of my sister Vicky's wedding the next afternoon. Two women were arranging flowers; the organist was practising; we put the orders of service somewhere we could find them, checked the layout of the building, agreed where people would sit. Vicky and her husband-to-be ran through the important parts of the ceremony while my father stood in the "giving away" spot, my mother watched, and I checked out what the ushers were supposed to do. We finished at about 8.50pm and went home.

At 9.20pm, a car bomb set by the IRA went off in St Mary Axe behind the church. It was apparently aimed at the Baltic Exchange building, or possibly at the Stock Exchange (and planted by some people who did not have an A to Z map-book of London). It killed three people. The organist and flower ladies were lucky to escape – masonry was falling and glass was flying. The church was badly damaged, and a police cordon was thrown around the whole area.

My older sister Penny and her husband and a cousin from Canada had come back to our house for a late dinner after the rehearsal. We were just finishing when my father rang: "Have you heard the news?"

"What news?"

"The IRA have blown up the church." This was too bizarre to comprehend. Why on earth would the IRA want to blow up the church? How could they have done so in the two hours since we left it? But it was so. I asked my father what he thought we ought to do. He was very matter-of-fact about it: "I suppose we shall have to find another church."

I have been to weddings where people are upset because the wine is a degree too warm or the flowers are just the wrong shade or Uncle George gets a little too drunk. Maybe it is easier to cope with a complete disaster than a minor annoyance. Anyway, we were all up early the next morning; the Vicar of St Helen's went out on foot to find a nearby church that was not booked for the afternoon, and reported back by about 8.30am that there was one in the Barbican we could use; we put in place a telephone cascade, and there was only one guest who was not present and correct at 3.00pm for the wedding. Being my most formidable aunt, she was presumably arguing with a policeman on the edge of the cordon that she really had to be allowed through.

I took two lessons from this. One is that it is unwise for people to hang around with me on a regular basis, as I will be the subject of an assassination attempt again sooner or later. The second is that real disasters – my brother dying, the hijack – give you a very good sense of proportion. All of us were sad for those who died, sad for the damage to St Helen's, but relieved that we were all unharmed and able to get on with a wedding.

Vicky also had her place in the Sunday papers – under the headline "Blast, it's my wedding day".

2000

In February 2000, an Afghan airliner was hijacked and brought to London's fourth airport at Stansted. Because the ensuing siege lasted for five days, there was time for journalists to dig out the old databases again. The papers contained lists of previous hijacks, including "mine" as having ended with a storming; and I received requests for comments.

The years had lowered my ratings, I found. In 1988, it was a television appearance on BBC *Breakfast Time*; by 2000, it was the drive-time programme on BBC Radio London, two lines in *The Daily Express* and a short piece in *The Scotsman*.

A friend sent me an e-mail to say that she had seen the report in the English paper, and was shocked to find that I had been in a hijack; I was equally shocked that she read the *Express*.

My six-year old daughter sat in the kitchen while I spoke to the interviewer on the telephone from the front room. She was disturbed to hear "Daddy *in* the radio" and thought it was a mean trick to play on her.

This incident followed very soon after the hijacking of an Indian plane to Kandahar in December 1999. It appeared that that first attack had resulted in concessions from the Indian government (whether that was actually the case or not, it was certainly the impression). It was followed by another hijack within weeks. Could these events possibly be related?

A KIND OF JUSTICE?

News of the gang

In spite of my contacts with the authorities through the various courses I presented, I found it very hard to get any hard information about what had happened to the hijackers. A year after the event, we heard that they were tried in Pakistan and sentenced to death. Then they appealed; while that was in progress, in August 1988 General Zia ul-Haq died in an apparent sabotage attack on his aircraft. It might be difficult for a Muslim country to put to death Muslim terrorists: there would be plenty of people who sympathised with them and supported them. In the wilder north of the country, we had seen graffiti saying "death to America" and plenty of posters of the Ayatollah Khomeini. We heard that the death sentences had been commuted to life imprisonment.

The rumours about who was behind the hijacking started almost immediately. Abu Nidal, responsible for a string of terrorist attacks through the 1970s and 1980s, was surely the one who gave the order . Some pointed the finger even then at Libya: the Abu Nidal Organisation was known to be used by Colonel Gadaffy, and it seemed very credible that Abu Nidal had been paid to hurt an American target after the Libyan bombings earlier in 1986. The ANO is also linked to the bombing of Pan Am flight 103 over Lockerbie on 21 December 1988, when 270 people died. Libyan security agents planted the bomb, but there is a strong rumour that the ANO supplied it.

At a presentation to the British Army Staff College in the mid-1990s, a Pakistani officer came up to me afterwards to express his heartfelt regret for what I had suffered in his country. He told me that he thought the terrorists had been executed. I tried to get confirmation from the Foreign Office, but no-one seemed to know. They passed out of my knowledge until 2001.

I was not called on for their trial in Pakistan. I was asked, however, to give evidence in London to a 1988 inquest into the death of a British citizen who died. This was Surendra Patel, listed on the official roll of casualties as an American. He must have had dual, or possibly triple, nationality. British law requires an inquest into Britons who die abroad, even if they do not live in the UK; so the coroner's court in north London investigated it, and held a brief hearing just after the start of the Kuwait Air hijacking.

I was amazed by the lengths to which the coroner's officers had gone to prove what seemed utterly obvious to me. That is not a criticism – they were doing their job very professionally and making sure that there were no loose ends. I was just surprised how much effort was involved in that. The main point that they were concerned to clear up was the assertion by the hijackers in their Pakistani trial that the fatalities had been caused by the commandos storming the plane, so my evidence that the commandos had not arrived until after the shooting finished was useful to the court. But the coroner's officers had also established that the bullets taken out of the dead man were from a Kalashnikov, and this weapon was not in issue to the Pakistani commandos or any part of the Pakistani military. I was able to say that I had seen the terrorists with Kalashnikovs, which I had identified as such soon after the event. The coroner's verdict drew the only possible conclusion: the terrorists killed him.

This was a quiet hearing in a safe location in urban London. I was glad not to have to catch a plane half-way across the world to bear witness against Muslim hijackers in a Muslim country. Sunshine and one of the other flight attendants, together with the Pan Am station chief Viraf Daroga, had to do that. They were in the front line on the day, and they seemed to be there still. I am told that the gang were physically in very good shape, intimidating, arrogant, full of themselves at the trial, making death threats against a journalist who dared to take a picture of them. There was no repentance, and they apparently did not feel cowed by the prospect of the justice that would be imposed on them by a Pakistani court. Nevertheless, they were convicted and sentenced.

2000

A sealed indictment of charges against the hijackers was returned by a grand jury in the District of Columbia in 1991. The US Department of Justice had never given up on the possibility of bringing the men to trial in the USA. In early 2000, Pakistani officials began to let it be known that their terms of imprisonment would soon come to an end. On June 19, the Federal Court in Washington DC granted the US government's request to "unseal the indictments", making the charges public. This effectively gave notice that the men were still wanted for the crime by the USA, even if they remained in jail in Pakistan.

2001

September 11, 2001: everyone has a story, even if it is only "where I was when I heard". One of my brothers-in-law was a flight attendant flying on United out of Boston, and my wife – his sister – spent a frantic afternoon trying to establish that he had not been on *that* flight. Terrorism happens to other people, but it also happens to us. He was safe, but of course he knew people who were not.

People said that I must have been terribly affected by the stories. I doubt if I was more affected than anyone else – it was a great deal different from my hijacking, and I think most people were so shattered that ranking the level of emotion is irrelevant. I was probably differently affected, though: I was in tears reading about the passengers phoning their loved ones to say goodbye, because I really felt I knew what that might be like.

Meanwhile, back in a Pakistani jail...

By coincidence (apparently), the man I knew as Abbas was released from jail in Pakistan in September 2001. He was given parole on condition that he left the country. He was originally from Jordan, and Jordan agreed to give him a passport. Pakistan deported him to Thailand, which was the country from which he had arrived in 1986. In Bangkok, he expected to board a plane for Amman; instead, he met the FBI, and found himself on the way to Anchorage (a small alphabetical difference, but he must have found it surprisingly chilly when he arrived). There is a whole other story to be told about this arrest, I feel – for example, I do not know whether he made his journey to Alaska in a seat or in a bag.

Someone drew my attention to this story when President Bush referred to the arrest in a speech on 25 September. It was the first confirmation I had had since the early 1990s of what had happened to the terrorists. Now it was clear: the death sentences had indeed been commuted, and the Pakistanis had decided that 15 years (including time before trial) was enough to qualify for parole. The other four were also eligible for release, and only required another country to give them papers and accept them.

There are many interesting questions about this story – whether there was an agreement between the US government and one or more of the other countries to make it possible for the arrest to take place; on what legal basis could a man who has served his term of imprisonment in Pakistan be arrested by American law enforcement agents in a third country and taken to the USA; whether Jordan or Thailand objected to the possible infringement of their sovereignty. What is clearest to me is that September 2001 was not a good time for the hijacker of an American plane to be at large in the world, particularly if he could be easily tracked. The Americans had presumably kept a close eye on what happened to these men, and had never given up the idea of bringing them to justice on American soil. President Bush was able to refer to the arrest in a speech on 25 September 2001, a small success in the opening of his war on terror.

Recently there has been a debate about "extraordinary rendition" – which seems to be, in essence, moving US prisoners about the globe to places where they will have fewer legal and human rights. This arrest and removal from Thailand seems to be slightly more respectable behaviour, but the legality of it still seems questionable.

At that time, his name was given as Zayd Hassan Abd Al-Latif Masud Al Safarini. This meant nothing to me – I had no idea which of the gang of four – or possibly five – this was. It was only much later that I was able to confirm that this mouthful referred to Abbas, and the other four remain in jail in Pakistan. They are apparently free to leave prison, as long as they then leave the country. They can only leave the country if another state will accept them. The only place willing to do so is the USA. They prefer to stay where they are.

2002

Following the arrest of Safarini, I received a series of letters from the US Department of Justice which – in the post-9/11 paranoia – were marked "irradiated". I suppose this was meant to be reassuring, but I found it disturbing. The gist was that he would be prosecuted in the USA, and the State would be pressing for the death penalty. At first, I thought that this was simply providing me with information; then, on 30 April 2002, they wrote to ask me whether I supported their request for execution. This was my reply (leaving out another brief summary of the story):

> You have asked me for my views and sentiments, and I hope that you will not mind if they take up a couple of pages. It is not easy to represent briefly what I regard as a complex issue. If my views are of any importance to the Court, I would like to take a little space to make them as clear as possible.

> This is a very difficult issue for me. During the hijack, I determined that I would not die frightened of these men, and I would not die angry with them. I was determined to forgive them. Afterwards, when I found to my surprise that I had not died, I found it hard to recreate the anger that I might have felt on my own behalf. In the end, it seemed that they did not do anything lastingly harmful to me.

> But then I visited in hospital a British woman who was caught in one of the grenade blasts, and the horror of what they did was brought home to me. For some years, I told classes at Hendon that I do not believe in the death penalty in general, and I would not want them dead for what they did to me, but I thought that justice demanded that they should die for what they did to the others.

However, that was before I was actually asked the question, with the possibility that my view would have some bearing on the outcome. In fact, I doubt if my view will have much bearing, because you will no doubt be taking views from a number of people, and there will no doubt be a general consensus one way or the other. But, for what it is worth, and for several reasons, I cannot bring myself to support the death penalty in this case. I would not consider it a terrible thing – I think that it would represent justice. I would not protest outside the prison against the penalty. But I would also not want to be one of those people who would queue up to press the button.

The first reason is that I am British, and we have not had the death penalty here since I was a small boy. I have been brought up a Christian, and I cannot quite accept that it is right for the State to kill a man, even if he has killed others. Although justice demands an eye for an eye, I believe that the State must rise above the justice of equal barbarity. But the USA has a different view and different laws, and so the fact that I am British affects only my views and sentiments, rather than being directly relevant to what you propose to do.

I am sure that, in this case, most of the important practical reasons for disapproval of the death penalty do not apply – I expect that you have got the right man, and that he definitely was responsible for the deaths of those passengers who died. This is not about the usual reservations that "if you kill the wrong man, you cannot reverse the punishment".

The second reason, which I feel very strongly, is that it seems unwise to create a martyr. I am sure that a balance has to be struck between the need to send a strong message to potential terrorists around the world, that the USA will pursue and will punish those responsible for terrorism, and the need to address the causes of terrorism and to lessen the eagerness of young Muslims to become terrorists. The trouble is that many young Muslims will not see the execution of this man as a terrible punishment to be feared, but something to be both aspired to – they will think he has gone straight to paradise – and to be avenged. It seems to me that the execution of a Muslim terrorist is like cutting off the hydra's head. There will be more, and more, and more. Imprisonment is not a satisfactory punishment from the point of view of justice, but it is less likely to have this effect.

The third reason is that I am uncomfortable with the legal basis on which he has been arrested, taken to the USA and put on trial. It may be that you can reassure me on this point, but I feel uneasy about it. As I understand it, he was tried and convicted in Pakistan, and I assume that he served his term. I do not fully understand how, in international law, he can be arrested outside the USA, taken to the USA, and put on trial again. If this is clearly in accordance with international law, I think it would be very useful for you to explain it very clearly to all concerned, so that once again there is no propaganda weapon that can be used against the USA. If the USA appears to be bending the rules in order to pursue Muslims, then Muslims will increase their sense of injustice and more will take up arms against all things American. For this reason, until I am put in possession of the facts about the legal basis of this trial, I could not call for the death penalty.

After this letter, we exchanged e-mails and agreed that if I was going to be in the USA, I would let the Department of Justice know and they would come to interview me. The Department did not provide me with any answers to the questions I raised, and I continued to feel uncomfortable about some of the legal issues involved.

*****

I was in the USA with my family in August 2002 when I saw a footnote in the paper: "Abu Nidal reported dead". It seems that he was found with gunshot wounds at his home in Baghdad, and may have been killed on the orders of Saddam Hussein, who was still in charge at that time. The databases were opened again, and the old annoying story about the storming of PA 073 by the commandos was trotted out.

I was amused by one of the sub-stories. The databases also contained the name and address of Abu Nidal's brother, who testily told the journalists that he hadn't seen the man for 40 years and why did people keep bothering him? Ah, but he would say that, wouldn't he...?

2003

The first opportunity to see the Department of Justice came in January 2003, when I had been booked to do a course on Value Added Tax in Stamford, Connecticut. This was a big deal for me: my first ever international course, a big client, and – by my modest standards – a very big fee. I was to fly out on Sunday, run the course from Monday to Wednesday, and receive a visit on Monday evening from two prosecutors from the Department together with two FBI agents. This was quite an exciting prospect, and I felt I had to explain to my client why so much law enforcement would be turning up at the hotel during the course.

On the Saturday, I got my things together ready for the trip – and could not find my passport. This was one of the worst days of my life (having described the two others earlier in this account – the day we heard that Peter had died, and the other one). I turned the house upside down, but it was not there. I had to ring up my client and tell him I would not be able to present the course. He was extraordinarily good about it, and agreed to do it himself, using material that I could provide over the internet. But the Department of Justice is closed at weekends, and I could only leave messages on an answering machine in the hope of stopping four senior law officers wasting their Monday going from Washington to Stamford and back.

The only thing that sustained me – just – was the thought that the last time I had lost my passport, it was because Abbas had it. However, there are limits to a sense of proportion, and I was fairly wrecked by the professional embarrassment, financial disaster and everything else.

The getting of a new passport turned into almost as much of an epic as the rest of this story, but it's not really relevant, so I will leave it out. I was surprised to find that it was possible to have a new one in my hand and be on a plane on Tuesday afternoon – the client said that it would be better for me to turn up and present one day out of three, than not to turn up at all. I was a little concerned that he simply wanted to wring my neck, and was being so nice about it on the phone so that I would actually come within wringing range.

My messages had managed to intercept the law officers at Washington airport on the Monday morning, and once I had established that I could come after all, they arranged for me to fly down to see them on the Thursday, after the course had finished. I had been through US airport security post-9/11, but there seemed to be extra checks for flights going to Ronald Reagan airport in the centre of Washington, and there was also a warning that if anyone got up in the half hour before landing, we would have to divert to Dulles (an hour's drive outside the city). As the flight from JFK only takes about 45 minutes, this was most of the flight. All the passengers seemed to be staring at each other waiting for someone to twitch.

The FBI were waiting for me at the airport (I have that in common with Safarini) and they drove me into central Washington to the offices of the Department of Justice. I met the prosecutors with whom I had been corresponding, Gregg Maisel and Jennifer Levy. I was debriefed one more time by them and two FBI men. I told them the story, as I had done to so many courses over so many years. At the end of it, to my surprise, Gregg produced a typewritten report of the interview I had given in my kitchen to the man from the US Embassy on the Wednesday after the hijack. He asked me to read it and see if I had anything to add, subtract or comment on.

It was a strange experience to re-read that completely raw account. There were things that I have added to the story over the years because I have found them out from other sources; things that I have remembered differently; things that did not occur to me when I was talking so soon after the event. After reading the statement, I said that I was sorry about the inconsistencies. "Oh no", said Gregg. "After nearly 18 years, I am amazed that it is so consistent." I suppose that someone who had not repeated the essence of the tale two hundred times in the meantime would be likely to have much bigger gaps.

I was concerned about a number of legal aspects of the forthcoming trial. I told the legal team that I would not support an application for the death penalty. I was worried about the concept of double jeopardy, and the legality of the way in which Safarini had been arrested on foreign soil – possibly kidnapped. In the most professional and gentle way, Gregg told me that what I thought about these things wasn't particularly relevant. What they wanted from me was information: my story. What the court did with that information was the court's concern, and it was not my responsibility.

I asked them who Safarini was, and they told me that they would ask the questions. Although they were not relying on me for identification evidence – they were quite confident of the identity of the man they were holding – it would not be proper for the prosecutors to be giving any information at all to a witness. This was frustrating, but at least I could see that they were doing everything very properly, by the book.

Then, half-way through our discussions, a thought suddenly penetrated the thickness of my brain. I asked them, "You aren't just taking a statement here, are you? You want me to go into the witness box at the trial."

"Oh yes, absolutely."

This had not occurred to me before, for some reason. I suppose it was the fact that they had surely such a lot of evidence anyway; or the fact that the Pakistanis had happily convicted the man without my help. I asked about the safety of witnesses in such cases.

They tried to reassure me: "We'll show you the courtroom in a minute. It's got bulletproof glass in it."

"And...afterwards?"

They looked blank. "Afterwards?"

That was what I was afraid of. But we had a discussion: they did not think (as they would say, wouldn't they) that there was any danger to witnesses in this sort of case. There was no history of revenge being taken on witnesses, and no likelihood that any individual would be considered sufficiently crucial to the case to be worth silencing in advance. Besides, it was unlikely that Safarini had many significant friends left at large who would or could do such a thing. They weren't worried.

I suppose that the prosecutor is at about as much risk as a witness, so it wasn't just my neck they were declaring safe.

We went to the courthouse and looked at one of the courtrooms – the one with the bullet-proof glass was in use, so we just had to make do with an ordinary one. Gregg pointed out where the jury would sit, the judge, the prosecuting counsel, myself as a witness.

I asked, "Where will the defendant be?"

"We can't tell you that" was the instant response. I thought that I would be able to work it out by process of elimination, as the defendant was likely to be the only Arabic-looking man and probably surrounded by burly guards, but they really didn't want to give me any information at all.

At that point, they were expecting preliminary arguments about the case to be heard in a few months, and the trial might happen either shortly before or shortly after the summer holidays. They were still expecting a full jury trial. They would keep in touch.

The arguments about the death penalty started in September 2002 with the defence team filing a motion that it would violate the "ex post facto" clause of the Constitution – at the time of the offence, the death penalty would not have been available for a crime committed overseas. The Department continued to argue about this, but the court delivered its opinion on 10 April 2003 that the defence team was correct. Arguments continued through the spring and summer, culminating in a plea bargain: Safarini would plead guilty to all the counts, and would accept a sentence of three consecutive lives plus 25 years (which is calculated at 160 years), and the government would drop the pursuit of the death penalty. Some bargain! The guilty plea was entered in court on December 16, 2003, and a sentencing hearing was set for May 2004.

Jamal

The world is full of coincidences. Later in 2003, and completely unconnected to any of these other events, I was contacted by a television producer, Roger, who said he was in touch with one of the gang still lingering in prison in Pakistan. Would I meet him to talk about the story? I would.

It seemed to me that Roger had a vision of a programme in which I would meet with this man and shake hands. Given that the man was still in jail, and would not leave it because the only country in the world that would have him was the USA, this seemed a little unlikely; but, to put it beyond doubt, I said that I would not take part in any such thing. The man is a murderer.

Roger told me the tale of Jamal Abdul Rahim. He had entered into correspondence with an Englishwoman from the north east, possibly someone who writes to prisoners in foreign jails as a humanitarian service. She passed on the contact to Roger because she thought he might be interested in the situation. The four remaining terrorists remain in a legal limbo, free on parole but unable to leave prison. They would not be allowed to stay in Pakistan, and they would only be allowed to leave if another country would agree to take them. As their countries of origin – three from Jordan, one from Libya – now seem unwilling, and no-one else will give them papers, they would rather stay in jail than risk almost certain arrest and transportation to face the wrath of America.

It is a peculiar situation, but I don't feel sorry for them. They were given life sentences, and they fully deserved them. If they would prefer to serve their life sentences in full in Pakistan, rather than take a brief period of parole and the likelihood of further imprisonment in America, then I am satisfied.

Roger showed me two pictures of Jamal, which meant nothing to me. I was glad I would not be relied on for identification evidence in Safarini's case, because the pictures showed two things very clearly – it was a long time ago to remember what the man looked like then, and he was likely to look very different now. After discussing the photos and the name with the flight attendants later, I believe that this is the man they knew as Ismail, and I called Ali – the young, aggressive one.

I told Roger I didn't mind him mentioning to Jamal that he had met me, as long as he did not give my name. A short while later, he forwarded a letter from Jamal to me. This is our brief correspondence:

Ali/Ismail/Jamal's letter to me: 20 October 2003 (verbatim copy of handwritten text)

Dear Sir

For a few months I have been in contact with Mr RB. He informed me about you. He agreed on my request to pass this letter to you. I shall be indebted to him if he does and to you if you kindly thoughtfully read.

I was one of the hijackers of ill fated Pan Am flight which was hijacked on the 5th of September, 1986. An event which you can't forget as it must had altered your life as you were one of most unfortunate passenger taken hostages on that fateful day.

I am aware that deep in your heart you must hate me because of what you had suffered as a result of the senseless hijack.

And like you I hate the 'me' I was.

I don't intend to justify to you an abhorred act of violence I took part in in the past. Simply because I can't. I don't believe in violence any more.

I have been in prison for more than seventeen years now and I have learned a lot.

I learned that I was fatally wrong. I was at the wrong place, at the wrong time hurting the wrong people. More ever, and most importantly, I learned that the religion I profess preaches peace and tolerance and not aggression and hatred.

Summarily, I wish you to know that I do regret and repent ever being one of the senseless hijackers almost two decades ago.

I do owe everyone who suffered as a result of the hijacking an overdue apology. My family, you and other victims of the Pan

Am hijack. My family was able to forgive me. And to you personally, I say I am sorry. And I hope that one day you will also be able to forgive me for sufferings and the hurt I caused to you directly and indirectly.

Yours truly, Jamal Abdul Rahim

My reply to him:

To: Jamal Abdul Rahim   8 December, 2003

RB has passed me the letter you wrote to me. When he told me about your letter, I did not intend to answer; but reading what you have written, I think that it deserves a reply. I hope that you will understand if I do not give you my name. I do not think that you have any wish to hurt me or my family, or any ability to do so, but I would rather not be identified.

First, let me say that I believe that your apology is heartfelt and genuine. I suppose some people will think that you are just saying sorry in the hope that you will get some better treatment somehow. I do not think that. Apart from anything else, there is nothing that I can do to help you, so there would be no point in your saying sorry to me unless you mean it.

You think that I must hate you, deep in my heart. I do not. The only thing I feel when reading your letter is sadness. I have long believed that you, and probably at least some of your colleagues on that day, were misguided by others into believing that what you did was just and right and would help the Palestinian cause. Those who knew that it was wrong and probably would not help were not there. Your life has been destroyed by the events of that day, just as much as the lives of those who were killed or injured, or the lives of the families who lost someone. The main difference is that you chose to be involved in a hijacking, and they did not. I feel great sadness for both sides.

There is a saying in my country, "do not let the sun go down on your anger": do not have an argument unsettled when you sleep. On that day, as I was waiting by the front door of the plane and expecting to be executed, I determined in my heart

167

that I would not die frightened, I would not die angry, I would not die hating you. I was determined that, if your leader (I do not know which of you is which) came down the stairs and said he was going to shoot me, I would offer to shake his hand. I don't know whether I could have done it, but after that, I was no longer afraid, because I felt that you could not take away my self-respect. I dismissed hatred from my heart on that day, and I have not felt it since.

But I have felt anger at what was done. It may have been someone else who put the guns and grenades in your hands, but it was you who used them. I know that your defence at trial suggested that Pakistani commandos storming the plane caused the casualties; I don't know if you believe that, but it is not true. The Pakistani commandos were practising elsewhere when the shooting started, and they did not arrive until after you and your colleagues had run out of ammunition. All the killing on that day came from the guns and grenades that you carried aboard the plane. That is the truth that you have to live with. I understand that you must find it hard, as you have said that you no longer believe in violence. That is part of the sadness, the fact that it is a terrible mistake, but it cannot be undone.

You write about forgiveness. For my part, I do not hold back forgiveness. I did not hate you on that day, and I have not done so since. But I cannot say that "you are forgiven" – there are so many others who may not forgive, and I cannot speak for any of them. In the end, I was lucky, because I lived and was not injured. There were plenty who had much worse to remember the day by, and they may not forgive.

I am sad that you are stuck in a jail, a life wasted by what happened more than 17 years ago. I do not see any way out of it for you. You may know that your colleague Zaid Hasan Abd Latif Safarini was taken to America, and he has apparently agreed to plead guilty to the charges that have been laid against him. I expect that means that he will accept a sentence of life imprisonment in the USA, and he is unlikely to be freed. I do not know if he has renounced violence.

I have an idea which you might like to think about. The sad fact is that every few days there is another suicide bombing in Israel. Another Palestinian kills himself and some Israelis; the Israeli army responds with destructive force against what they see as the source of the attack; when the Israelis retaliate, there will be another suicide bomber, and it goes on and on and on with no apparent hope of an end. The circle of violence does no-one any good, and there is some right and enormous wrong on both sides.

You were once the sort of man who would be recruited to be a suicide bomber; but you now know better. I wonder if there is any way in which you could pass on your lesson to those who are being recruited now. I don't know how you could do it; I think it would require enormous courage, because there are plenty of people who would not want such a message to be passed on, and would take any measures they could to stop you. But if you could persuade a handful of people who would have become suicide bombers not to do so, you might save as many lives as were lost on 5 September 1986.

I leave you to think about that. I have no idea how it could be achieved, or whether you would consider doing it. I suppose the Americans might be interested in discussing such a thing, although they are most likely to be interested in discussing putting you on trial. Maybe the Palestinian authority would be interested, or even the Israelis. Someone speaking peace in the Middle East seems so unusual that no-one may know what to do about it.

In the Christian Bible, Jesus says "there is more joy in heaven over one wrongdoer who changes his heart and says sorry, than there is over ninety-nine righteous men who have no need of a change of heart". I am not a churchgoing Christian, but I believe that those are wise and true words. Maybe there is something in them for you.

Further reply from Jamal, dated 15 January 2004

Dear Sir

I was glad to receive your letter in response to mine. You can't imagine what that meant to me. It was kind of you to respond and share some of your feelings with me, though I was a cause of your anguish, pain and anger.

Nevertheless, I hope one day you'll be able to put the past behind you and then maybe I might be able to call you with your first name.

As you understood rightly, the purpose of my apology has no ulterior motives. I did that because this is the proper thing to do. More ever, that apology wasn't prompted by what was happening with Safarini in USA. In fact this had been on my mind for a long time now, but I lacked the means to do so. When I mentioned this first to Roger he suggested a public apology on a certain website. However, I believed an apology should be personal.

Maybe a public apology should come from those who used me and sent me to Pakistan, from the unrepenting godfathers of violence.

I am not aware if you still remember me vividly. I do remember you very well, though.

Here, I want to assure you that I was not your would have been executioner. Nor was I aware of the first execution that took place on that fateful day. In fact no executions were on the cards. However Safarini who is in USA custody now and who led the hijacking acted individually. Myself, I was the youngest. I was exactly seventeen years old on that day. Anyhow, this doesn't exonerate me in many eyes. Still, it is better to show remorse than be morbidly and senselessly defiant and express pride.

I speak for myself only. Some people never learn, however. Violence got us nowhere in the past and won't now, nor in the future.

Really, it does not matter much who was responsible for all the atrocities on that day. The fact is, had there been no hijacking, there would had been no bloodshed. I don't wish to discuss now the events of that day. But believe me, very few know the sad truth. Things could have been worse and uglier.

You are right, none of the past mistakes could be undone. But we learn and pass our knowledge to others, in order not to see them committed again. Still stopping others is not an easy task. It is like mission impossible. The bitter fact is, as long as there's injustice and hope does not gleam, people resisting are bound to go extreme. Unfortunately, there will always be 'ticking' suicide bombers. There will be people who 'let the sun go down' on their anger. And in the meantime precious lives will be lost when second class/'hand' failed leadship set these suiciders off.

Personally, I am in the Palestinian peace camp. And, given a chance I shall be active in that field. There is a lot I can do and contribute. Despite the lunacy prevailing in the middle east, we have many forums preaching tolerance and accommodation. And I believe the day won't be far when we will have peace. An everlasting one.

I have a few ideas of my own. Even being hunted by the Americans will not deter or make me change. However, I hope I'll be able to devote time to the handicapped in memory of a friend who died last year. She had devoted her whole life unrelentlessly to the cause of handicapped. And of course, I wish to work for peace in Palestine. Beside joining in efforts of enabling individual reconciliations on both the sides. I have to start somewhere. That is a reason why I wrote to you.

With best wishes

Yours, Jamal

Jamal's repentance may be genuine now, but Sunshine's description of him is chilling: *"Ismail, if he had been the leader, we would all be dead now"*. Whether he has changed or not, he was probably the worst of them all on 5 September 1986.

2004

In January 2004, the Department of Justice contacted as many of the victims of the hijacking as could be found, and asked us all if we wanted to come to the sentencing hearing. If we wished, we could address the court.

I had very mixed feelings about this. I had concerns about double jeopardy; the Americans could be argued to have violated the sovereignty of other countries in arresting the man, and also in trying him. I was unhappy with the war on terror, and the way in which the actions of America seemed likely to increase the antagonism between westerners and Muslims. I was worried that they might make a martyr out of him – or give some extremist mullah the opportunity to present him as one.

It would also be a long way to go for a trial whose outcome I was sure I would not influence at all. He had made his plea bargain: he would be sent down for life, or three lives. What difference would it make for me to speak, or listen?

In the end, I decided that I had to go. Presenting to courses on a regular basis has made the hijack such a part of my life that I could not simply ignore this. It would be very feeble to have to tell the next course that I could have gone to the sentencing proceeding but decided not to. And, I suppose, I wanted to see what he looked like.

Initially, I thought I would go on my own. Kathy wanted to come with me, but I felt nervous about leaving our children without one of us to look after them. I suppose I was worried, irrationally, that something might happen to me. If it did, I did not want it to happen to Kathy as well. She thought that I was cutting myself off from her, and it caused some strain between us: I could not easily or clearly describe why I felt that I needed to go to Washington without her.

In the end, it was going to see the film *Lost in Translation* that settled the matter. I realised that I needed her to be there – the film reminded me how being alone in a foreign city for even a routine trip is grim, and being alone through the sentencing hearing would be intolerable. The week before the hearing, the Department of Justice rang to say that they had found a little extra in the budget to pay for her ticket if she could come; we found some friends who were willing to take both our daughters for the inside of a week; and on a Tuesday morning we set off at six o'clock in the morning to catch a plane to Washington DC. We live only twenty minutes' drive from London's Heathrow airport, so six o'clock is good enough for an 8.30am flight.

Paranoia set in when the plane taxied to the end of the runway in the usual long Heathrow aircraft queue, then taxied back to the terminal building. Something wrong with something, they would try to replace it; we sat for a while, then we were offloaded and told we would all be catching the next flight. United Airlines were very efficient and pleasant about all this, but it was a little galling to have left the house at six o'clock and take off at midday.

As a result, we were late for the start of proceedings in Washington. The other people attending had arrived by lunchtime, had a briefing in the hotel where most of us were staying, and had been taken to the Federal courthouse in a bus for a rehearsal. When we arrived we had a phone number to ring and were asked to come down by taxi as soon as possible. We were greeted by a young man who was probably hardly born in 1986 – he was in charge of the travel and accommodation for all the witnesses, and he was busy juggling a large number of possible problems. We were impressed with how well he coped and how calm he stayed throughout the next two days.

We entered the back of the courtroom and slipped into the public seats. In the centre of the court, in front of the judge's bench, stood Gregg Maisel. He was going through a Powerpoint presentation on a large screen, explaining what he would say in the hearing the next day. Jennifer Levy was seated nearby, together with a few other officials unknown to me.

Gregg pointed out the various features of the courtroom, and now he wasn't shy about identifying the defendant: "He'll be the one in the orange jumpsuit." I suppose that this is the difference between a sentencing hearing and a trial – the Department didn't have to worry about proving anything. If we had all been there as witnesses in a trial, this rehearsal would have been completely out of order. This was a good thing: if the authorities had been required to keep us all at arm's length, I think quite a few of the witnesses would have gone to pieces. It was clear that several of us were already finding the emotion hard to deal with, even without Safarini in the room.

When Gregg had finished, there were questions from the floor. Some last minute details were changed, for example it was decided that the witnesses would sit in the witness box and address the court and the defendant, rather than standing at a lectern in the centre and addressing the judge. That would be a little more relaxed, not least because we would be further away from Safarini.

I looked at the people sitting around us and half-recognised one or two of them – after all, it had been a long time since meeting them for such a short time. Some people obviously knew each other, but I was feeling surprisingly withdrawn. I had told this story so many times to so many people – but I was full of nerves at the prospect of telling it to the people whose story was mixed up with mine. Kathy and I joined the others in a bus back to the hotel. We hardly exchanged any words with anyone that evening, and went out to dinner before getting an early night.

Nerves and jet-lag combined to wake me up in the small hours. I realised that I could not just sit and tell the tale as I normally do. I would have to have a script; I should say what was relevant to the court, not what was relevant to hostage negotiators. I should stick to my own experience and leave out anything that I had added to the story over the years. I should keep it down to about 20 minutes. It probably took me a couple of hours, sitting outside the bathroom in order not to wake Kathy, to come up with something I thought would do.

Over breakfast in the hotel, a formidable Indian lady fixed me with a stare and a jabbing finger. "I hate you!" she exclaimed. I looked a bit surprised at such hostility. "You haven't changed a bit. How dare you?" Then she grinned. This was Sunshine, who has a wicked sense of humour to go with the courage and ingenuity she showed during the hijack. She explained that she had felt awful during the day, knowing that she had put me at the head of the queue – and she had been greatly relieved to see me alive afterwards.

There wasn't much time for conversation, as the bus took everyone to the courthouse at 8.45am for a 10.00am start. We all had to be processed through security both at the entrance to the building and at the door to the court. Checking the witnesses for concealed weapons was probably more for the personal safety of Safarini than anyone else.

I expect we were all waiting impatiently to see him – the cause of so much misery. When he entered the room, dressed in his boilersuit and flanked by two heavy-set men who never took their eyes away from him over the next two days, it was almost a disappointment to me. I would not have recognised him in the street. I suppose the last 18 years had been harder for him than for me. He certainly looked older, heavier, sadder. He could no longer have cut the imposing figure he did on the day of the hijack. Stripped of his gun and his bravado, he was pathetic.

The full transcript of the sentencing proceeding is available on the internet: there is the presentation given by Gregg Maisel, then the statements from some 25 people who were affected (see

for the details). Some were on the plane; some lost family members; some were injured; some had been too young really to remember; some had been too young, but remembered only too clearly. I will not repeat what they said – that was their story, and if you are interested in it, you can find it out. I have included a very few extracts in my account of the end of the hijack, because without them the story is incomplete: like me, you would not fully understand how awful it was. But I have only related a very small fraction of what we heard over those two days.

It was striking that some of those who spoke said that they had never been able to talk about it before. They had kept it all to themselves, not telling their family or friends what it had been like. I realised how lucky I had been to have the opportunity. A whole family spoke one after another – the mother and two children who were on the plane, the father and two more who had waited at home. When they prepared their statements for the hearing, the children e-mailed them to their parents, even though they lived in the same house – they still could not bear to speak of it, even to each other.

I also realised how lucky I had been on the day, all over again. I had been so used to telling the story as something from which I was able to walk away: I could put jokes in it. These stories were raw and painful and brought tears to the eyes. I scribbled on my handwritten script – I had to make many last minute changes to make sure what I said was appropriate.

Sunshine spoke second, and she crackled with electric hostility. It was clear she despised and hated Safarini. I heard for the first time how he had taunted Rajesh Kumar as he begged for his life, asking "Are you a man?" before shooting him. Sunshine threw the words back at him. Without his gun, he was nothing.

The great majority of the witnesses were in favour of the death penalty, even though that was not what the proceeding was about. We were in the presence of the judge who had decided it was not available; the State had agreed to settle for three life sentences and 25 years, with no prospect of parole. I had the impression that many of them would have been happy to settle the matter there and then with a length of rope and a handy tree. One mild-mannered academic, whose father died, said "We the victims would like him to be torn to pieces, and the pieces fed to the hyenas; but we respect the rule of law." Lucky, that.

I did not feel the same way. I was with the small minority who would not have him executed, for reasons which I had explained in my letter to Gregg Maisel and which I explained further in my statement to the court. But I could not criticise those who wanted his blood. The trouble is that there is no justice: letting him live is not justice, but killing him is not really justice either. As soon as he carried out his murders, there could be no justice for any of those affected. There would be the rule of law, and there could be revenge, but nothing that would put right the wrong.

After relating the main facts of what happened to me, I did my best to put my thoughts about the event, the aftermath, and my reaction to it into appropriate words. The judge wanted to know what the victims, the survivors, had been through. I was acutely aware that most of the other people who spoke had expressed anger and pain, and I did not want to suggest that I thought they were wrong to do so. This is the conclusion of my address to the court :

> I want to say something about the effect on me afterwards. This is very strictly just about me, I don't expect anyone else to feel the same, and I am just one of many. For two years afterwards, the hijack was always on my mind – I would think about it every day. Not in any great fear and trembling, but it would always be running over and over in the background. I didn't have many nightmares – maybe three or four.

> Since then, I am probably more paranoid than I otherwise would be – I expect bad things to happen to me, because my passport is the one that will always get picked. But when bad things do happen, I am probably better at dealing with them than I otherwise would be. What I want to say is that he has not made me into a victim. I have had seventeen and a half years that I never expected to have, and I am still counting, and I know better than many how precious each day is. I have had the opportunity to do some useful work telling courses for hostage negotiators what it's like on the inside of a siege. So in my life – just my life – I have been lucky, and the impact of this event has been positive, at least in the long term.

> During the hijack, when I was expecting to die, I made up my mind that I would not die hating him, or angry with him, or frightened of him. It is perhaps a bit old-fashioned, but I had determined to offer to shake his hand if he decided to shoot me. I don't know if I could have done it, and from what I have heard today perhaps he would not have let me, but after I had decided that, I believed he could not take away my self-respect, and I wasn't really frightened of him any more. I suppose I forgave him then, just for me, and I cannot unforgive him now.

> But I cannot forgive him for the others. I have no business speaking for the 21 others who haven't had those extra years, and for the many more for whom those years have been hard and bitter. Like Gopal, I have a much-loved wife; like Prabhat, I

have a much-loved father; like Aneesh, I have a much-loved younger sister. If it had happened to them, I do not think I would be able to forgive, even if they had survived. I know how lucky I was to escape without an injury that would be a daily reminder. I doubt if I could forgive him then. My little piece of forgiveness has nothing to do with justice. I know that this court will try to bring justice for everyone, and I don't think justice has any business forgiving him at all.

Sir, I have a suggestion. If a tape could be made of the statements made in this court today, and played to him in prison, then that would be punishment indeed. If he could listen to what we have heard today and feel nothing, then he truly would not be human.

Looking at him here now, I am just sad. What a waste. He may have been misled by those above him in his organisation, he may have had some justice in his cause, but he has ruined the lives of scores of other people, and he has ruined his own life. I am only concerned that what is done with him can't be used as an excuse for others to carry on the circle of violence – again, just for myself, I was relieved that this proceeding is not about the death penalty, because I think that then some people would elevate him to the status of a martyr, and he doesn't really deserve such a status, even in the minds of twisted people. He is a coward.

If somehow in the rest of his life he could find some remorse, he could perhaps do something to persuade potential hijackers and suicide bombers that it's a senseless, useless and evil waste, and it undermines any justice in their cause, and it will never bring success to their cause, then I suppose he might still make something good of his life, even if he can never undo the terrible wrong he did before.

We heard statement after statement, witness after witness, for a day and a half. It was almost overpowering, intensely emotional. The prosecutors and their support staff told us that people were coming in from other parts of the building just to watch this extraordinary remembrance, this recollection of Safarini's evil being laid out before him while he sat, for most of the time impassive, with an interpreter whispering in his ear.

The judge showed great respect and sympathy for the survivors. We were referred to from time to time as "victims", but I don't like the word. We were all hurt in one way or another, but we all survived. I don't think we should allow ourselves to be turned into helpless victims, either by the likes of Safarini or by the attention of the law or the media. I believe we can take control again once the shooting is over, even if for some it is a slow and painful process.

At times, it almost seemed like a group therapy session presided over by the judge. There were murmurs of support from the gallery, and some heckling of the other side, that would probably not be tolerated in a normal hearing. I'm sure that everyone who was present must have found the experience moving, and I hope that everyone who had been involved found it helpful. I expect that those who would have found it too much stayed away – those who came were probably the stronger ones.

*****

At lunchtime on the first day, several of the witnesses lined up on the courthouse steps in the sunshine to speak to a TV crew from CNN. We spoke about what had happened and what was happening. But we were not sufficiently interesting for the evening news; this was an old story. There was a summary on the CNN website, and reports in the following day's newspapers – all of them refreshingly accurate.

*****

Just before lunch on the second day, we heard from one of the bravest men present – the prison chaplain who was prepared to stand up and speak on behalf of Safarini. There was a near-tangible hostility towards him, and I had to go up and shake his hand afterwards, because I thought he had spoken well in difficult conditions and deserved respect. I will reproduce his address, as I think it is interesting.

Your Honour, Judge Sullivan, survivors and family members of Pan Am 73, ladies and gentlemen, my name is Father Michael Bryant. I am a Catholic priest. And I have been the chaplain at the District Jail for 24 years. My background is that of a pastoral counsellor and a licensed mental health therapist.

I've been present throughout the sentencing hearings, listening and deeply saddened by the sheer volume of suffering associated with this atrocious event. I have read the painful accounts of the survivors and their horrifying memories, recounted in page after page of unspeakable horror in the written impact statements. And I was particularly saddened when I read the story of a mother who laid across her children in the dark and felt blood on their clothing and she did not know at that time whether it was their blood or someone else's.

I listened to statements of paralysing fear, paralysing fear of passengers who endured so many hours the dread of who might be next to die. The sheer terror, the loss, the sense of loss, the sense of powerlessness, the sense of helplessness, the rage and the anger. I thought, as I listened yesterday and today, that in a very real way I was on sacred ground. And I prayed for the many with so many wounded lives and so many painful memories.

My reason for coming to court today is to offer some insight into the mind and into the heart of Zayad Safarini, who I've come to know during his two and a half years in the District Jail.

One of the efforts of the chaplain service is to try to help prisoners and their families maintain contact while they are incarcerated. And it was in this context that I first met Mr Safarini. He had not spoken with his mother in a very long time and I helped him make initial contact with her in Jordan. Periodically, I did assist him in calling his family, not knowing at the time who he was or what he had done.

Zayad Safarini's demeanour when he came to the office was always respectful and unobtrusive. He was quiet, he was unassuming, he was subdued in manner. He was never insistent or demanding. Most of the time he was sad and depressed and I knew that he was on medication. The few times I saw Zayad smile and animated was when he spoke with his mother.

After many months of coming to the office and occasionally being able to call his family, I began to spend time sitting with him. Gradually I came to understand who he was. And then I visualised and recalled the television report of the news account of the passengers. Specifically, the passenger who was pushed from the door of the plane. That came to my memory years later. And as we talked, I was initially taken aback by the sheer number of people who had died or were injured. And for a time, I could not believe I was sitting in the presence of a person who was responsible for this horrific event.

As he continued to share his story, he never looked up, he always looked down. There were long pauses between words and sentences, his lips quivered. It indicated to me the pain associated with memories of what he had done. And he said to me in a broken voice, "I wish I were dead". I believe Zayad Safarini is overwhelmed when he visualises what he has done. I believe Zayad is frequently tormented by the memories of his deeds.

On that day in 1986, Zayad believed he was going to die on that airliner. He never considered having to live with the horror of his actions years later. On another occasion, he told me, "I am not the man I was then". I asked him if he wanted me to pray with him as our talk ended that day. I asked him if he wanted forgiveness, and he acknowledged he did. And as we prayed for God's healing for those who live with open wounds from this event, we also prayed for God's forgiveness upon him.

As I continued to listen, I began to see and hear a broken human being who now, 18 years after the fact, is, in my belief, deeply remorseful and contrite for what he has done. I believe further that he is no longer that young zealot of almost two decades ago. He is no longer a merciless terrorist threatening defenceless people.

From what I have heard and what I have seen, Zayad Safarini is a man deeply contrite and pained for causing so much horror in the lives of so many innocent people. And I also believe that God has forgiven him. And now Zayad wants to find words and asks your forgiveness.

In the jail, Zayad Safarini is not perceived as a threat or a danger by the administration or the correctional staff. After he was there a few months, he was put in open population. He attends Moslem services every Friday.

I would just like to close, if I may, with a few reflections. All great faith traditions believe that every person is made in the creator's image and is therefore sacred. No stoppable person's actions, no matter how inhuman, can take away their humanity as it is God-given. Punishment is a legitimate response to wrongdoing, but if it's punishment for punishment's sake alone, then it approaches retaliation. Punishment must be balanced with mercy to bring the reform of the sinner. If there is no mercy, if there is no compassion, then there's little hope for anyone.

I would like to respectfully share with you a way to find healing and peace, recognising that many in this room may not, and understandably so, have the same approach, finding healing and peace through forgiveness. Bishop Desmond Tutu of South Africa said when he was conducting the truth and reconciliation hearings in the aftermath of the apartheid atrocities, said, "There can be no future without forgiveness".

Ghandi said, "Hate the sin, love the sinner".

Martin Luther King said, "In the face of years of brutal racist behaviour in this country, the old law about an eye for an eye leaves everyone blind".

And again, we must maintain the capacity to forgive, for he who is devoid of the power to forgive is devoid of the power to love. There is some good in the worst of us and there's some evil in the best of us. When we discover this, we are less prone to hate our enemies.

And Jesus said from the cross, "Father, forgive them, for they do not know what they do". And again, "As I have forgiven you, so you must forgive one another".

My prayer is for each of you that you will find healing and peace.

There were a number of mutterings during this speech. It is, of course, the chaplain's part to talk about forgiveness; but forgiveness is not really what a sentencing hearing for a mass murderer is about, and there was very little of it at large in the room. The atmosphere was even more hostile when Safarini himself sat in the witness box to read his own statement. I think this section is also worth reproducing. Judge Sullivan may not have thought the death penalty was available, but that was clearly on purely legal grounds, and there is no doubt he had as much contempt for what Safarini had done as any of the survivors.

Safarini initially stood at the podium with his interpreter and spoke in Arabic, with the interpreter translating, and then read a statement in English. In what follows, 'Interpreter' means the interpreter speaking for herself, and 'Safarini' was his words translated by the interpreter. 'Defence' is Safarini's lawyer. This is what is recorded in the transcript of the court's proceedings (some of the English reflects the difficulty of translating speech as it happens):

Judge	Mr Safarini, would you like to come to the podium? Would you like to turn the podium around?
Interpreter	No, I have my own microphone, Your Honour.
Judge	I'm sorry, I was talking to him. Mr Safarini, would you like to turn the podium around so you could address the survivors?
Interpreter	He's saying, "I want to face Your Honour".
Judge	All right.
Safarini	Good afternoon. I initially wanted to address you in English, but in the Arabic language I can express myself

better. At the beginning I would like to express my remorse, certain sorrow. I am very, very, very sorry.

Judge	Would you like to turn to the victims and the survivors and express your sorrow to them directly?
Interpreter	He's going to try, Your Honour.
Judge	I'm not forcing you. I'm just asking you. You wanted to express your sorrow to me. That's fine. I'm not a victim. I'm not a survivor. I wasn't there. These people were there. They are family members of people who were there.
Interpreter	He says, "I would like to face Your Honour".
Judge	All right. So is that, no, you would not like to turn and speak to the victims? Would you like to sit at the... that's fine. Thank you, Marshal.
Defence	I had told him that I would stand next to him.
Judge	If you would like to stand next to your client, that's fine with me, if it's all right with the marshals. Sure, go ahead.
Safarini	At the beginning, I would like to start with expressing my remorse and sorrow. I was sorry from the very beginning, but after I read the statements of the victims, that added to my pain. And after I heard in court your statements, that added to my pain. I am really sorry for all my actions. I initially wanted to address the Court because I didn't – I am somewhat reluctant to face the victims in this sad incident.
Judge	Let me ask you a question. Why are you reluctant to face the victims?
Safarini	No, there is no reason why – there is no reason why, Your Honour.
Judge	There is no reason what?

184

Interpreter	He does not want to face the victims – there is no special – he's saying, "I'm facing them now". He said it in English, Your Honour.
Judge	All right.
Safarini	Now I would like to address Judge Sullivan and request the victims and the families of the victims to listen to me if they so desire. I am not going to ask you for forgiveness because I have suffered quite a lot.
Judge	You haven't suffered as much as these people have, sir. By no stretch of the imagination have you suffered as much as they have. You've heard their stories. They're still suffering and they're going to suffer continuously for the rest of their lives. You think your suffering is equal to theirs?
Safarini	No, Your Honour, I do not think so. Shall I continue? [*To be fair to Safarini, I think that is what he was trying to say – he did not want to ask the victims to take pity on his suffering, because it was of no consequence. But it was an unfortunate turn of phrase and it's not surprising the judge jumped on it.*]
Judge	Sure.
Safarini	But I would like them to know that I did listen to them and read their statements and I feel their pain and their sufferings. I am sorry for what has happened to them and for those that they love. I know I am sorry for all what they're suffering and I know that their sufferings are to continue for the rest of their lives. And I want them to know that all this pain, I take the responsibility for all this pain that they are suffering. And I wish that all your pains and aches would…
Interpreter	I'm getting a little bit nervous. I'm sorry.

185

Safarini   …would heal and I take responsibility for all this pain.
                And my sorrow is from the depth of my heart. If you do
                not believe that I am a person who has a heart, I can
                understand that and I would accept that. And I strongly
                believe that if anybody has exerted or done that to me,
                that person would be having a very thick heart and does
                not have any weight or meaning or understanding of
                humanity. I know that it is very difficult that you would
                believe in my truth and my words would not have any
                value. But this is all what I possess. Once again, I do
                express my remorse and sorrow and I do strongly wish
                that all those who are suffering, that their hurts and
                feelings would heal. And I think of them all the time.
                And I remember all what has happened in Pakistan as if
                it happened yesterday.

                I strongly express my remorse and sorrow and that was
                wrong. I'm aware of the fact that those people who
                were on the plane really suffered and I bear the
                responsibility for these actions. This is a horrible
                incident. And what I feel today words cannot express
                the extent of my feelings.

                At the beginning, I used to have dreams every night
                about these actions and incident. And I still get
                nightmares of this incident. And I abruptly get up out of
                my sleep in fear. But I would like to express to you that
                I wish I had died on the plane. I don't say that so that
                you would feel sorry towards me. I am telling you that
                because if that person had done these horrible actions
                towards me, I would wish that that person would suffer
                in pain.

                That's why I am telling you that I am suffering and I
                have no hope. This is a horrible matter that I am living
                through. I am not enjoying my life and I don't feel any
                happiness. And I sit in my cell and have no hope and no
                feeling of life. I know that when I die that I'm going to
                be by myself without ever seeing my family.

Safarini I also would like to bring to your attention two matters. That I do not hate the United States. I admire this country tremendously, their traditions and their thinking and the freedom in this country. When I was incarcerated in Pakistan, I used to read a lot about the United States. It appeared to me that it is full of light and it was full of … it was bright and full of light and full of freedom and ever twinkling.

And I would like to tell you that when I committed these actions, I did not do that as a drive on account of my religion. At the beginning when I got involved with this organisation it was my understanding that I was extending a helping hand to the Palestinian people. I believed that I was living a dream for a country, a homeland. On that account, myself and my family … so that myself and my family would go back to our homeland.

Now I quite believe that the organisation that I was a part of, this is not their aim. Now I know that I was used and so were the others. And I was at fault and I was wrong and so were the others that the force I was using was serving the Palestinian cause. I was at fault. I was wrong. And the victims that fell were innocent people. They had no relation or connection to the Palestinian cause. I am not expressing an explanation to give you reason for what happened because that is impossible. I am sorry, I am remorseful, and thank you.

Judge When the plane was taken over, did you think that the Palestinian cause justified that type of activity?

Safarini In the past, this was my understanding.

Judge At the time the plane was taken over and at the time that innocent and defenceless men and women and children were murdered, do you really believe that your cause justified that type of conduct?

Safarini No, Your Honour.

Judge	At the time it was significant, though?
Safarini	I was brainwashed.
Judge	Into believing that your conduct and activities were justified then on behalf of the Palestinian cause?
Safarini	Yes, Your Honour, at that time, yes.
Judge	All right. Is there something else you'd like to say? My understanding is you'd like to make a statement in English now, is that correct? Before you do that, who brainwashed you?
Safarini	The organisation I was a part of.
Judge	So you were told that this type of conduct or that type of conduct was justified then.
Safarini	Yes, Your Honour.
Judge	And you believed it?
Safarini	In the past, yes.
Judge	How could any cause justify the killing of defenceless men, women and children?
Safarini	I admit that that was wrong.
Judge	All right.

Safarini then read out an English translation of what he had spoken in Arabic through the interpreter. It says much the same thing, but he managed to get it out without the judge interrupting him again.

It is not a bad statement, if it is sincere. It says what it ought to say; it cannot make anything right, but it contains the right amount of abject remorse and hopelessness. I was inclined to accept it at face value, but Sunshine was not. She had been a witness at the trial in Pakistan, when the hijackers were certainly not showing any regret – they were clearly proud of what they had done at that time, full of arrogance and insolence, and very frightening for the witnesses. She also picked up a smile on his face when she was giving evidence in Washington, and thought that he was still mocking her. She may have been right. I could not tell what he was really like in 1986, and I still cannot.

*****

After Safarini spoke, the judge did something apparently unprecedented and completely out of order: he asked the survivors and victims if they had anything to add. The legal personnel called this "a rebuttal of the defendant's statement", and they were very excited about it. Several witnesses made further statements, most of them questioning his sincerity or pointing out that it made no difference – it was all very well to be sorry now, but the dead were still dead. I joined the queue and spoke briefly again.

> I don't know whether I believe him or not. I said yesterday I never knew then. But I feel that if it is true that he feels remorse, if there is any element of truth in that, then his life sentence will be terrible whether he lives it in solitary or whether he lives it with other people. Because he will have the words of all the people who sat here in his head for the rest of his life.

> As I said yesterday, and am going to say it again now, if he could be used in some way to get this message across to the other people who may have their own twisted reasons, who may be misled in their own way to go out and kill other people, then that would be a powerful force for good. I know he's done terrible wrong and he can never undo that. But if only he could do something, if only he could do something so that other people won't be sitting in this courtroom in some future year, then maybe he would deserve not to be in solitary confinement.

> That was one thing. The only other thing I would have to say is, as I said yesterday, I only speak for myself. And I quite understand why many people would want him to be locked in the darkest dungeon. But not for me. Not for me.

Gregg had clearly hoped to wrap the whole thing up in one day, although up to two days had been allotted, and everyone's travel and accommodation was fixed to send us home on Friday. The judge told everyone to take as long as they liked, and those who for 18 years had not had the opportunity or the inclination to talk made up for it. The survivors spoke in turn for the whole of the first afternoon and most of the second morning; then there were the representations from the defence, including Safarini's statement; and then we had "the last word", before some legal discussion about the sentence.

This may sound surprising, given that there was a plea bargain. The judge started to talk about the minimum term before a parole hearing, and Gregg jumped in immediately to point out that the terms of the bargain included no possibility of parole. But the prosecution also picked up on a suggestion from one of the witnesses that Safarini should serve his term in solitary confinement: the judge said that such a decision was up to the prison department, rather than the court, but after hearing all that he had heard, he would indeed recommend it. The defence protested that this was more than was necessary for someone who posed no threat and who had expressed remorse, but their arguments got nowhere with the judge.

As far as I know, Safarini is now held in an underground facility in Florence, Colorado, called "Super Max". I occasionally receive computer-generated letters telling me about his progress – this is a form which is presumably sent to registered victims of crime, with a list of check boxes which is surely funnier than it is supposed to be. The same form will apparently arrive to tell me whether my "perpetrator" has:

- been moved to a different prison;
- applied for parole;
- been released;
- died;
- escaped.

The postman will be bringing them for 160 years.

What I learned in America

I learned many parts of the story that I had not previously known. Safarini's background was explained: he had joined the Abu Nidal Organisation several years earlier, and had been sent on his first significant mission in 1983. He went to Malta with orders to assassinate a PLO representative (presumably for not being sufficiently radical). He planned carefully for three days, and then killed – the wrong man. This is, of course, tragic; but it seems that his terrorist career was a continuous farcical failure.

I discovered that the man on the runway with the megaphone was Viraf Daroga, the Pan Am station chief, and not a Pakistani official as I had always imagined. Mr Daroga was the first person to speak in the hearing. I think I owe him my life.

I found out which of the flight attendants had done what – I always knew that Sunshine had hidden the passports, but I was now able to identify and talk to the woman who had stood in the doorway with the megaphone, and the one who had dealt with the emergency of the smoke alarm going off in the toilet. Four of the flight attendants came to the hearing, and they are still an extraordinary group – bright, caring, full of courage, and – in Sunshine's case at least – not a little scary.

I heard about the trust that was set up in memory of Neerja by her family, making annual awards to women in India who have "done their duty, come what may". Her brother Aneesh gave me a booklet about the trust – it is filled with accounts of how she died of the wounds she suffered while trying to help the passengers escape, and with pictures of a remarkably beautiful young woman.

At one break in the hearings, I noticed an older Indian couple looking at me and whispering to each other. I went across to greet them, and they said, delighted, "It *is* him! It's the hippy man!" They told me the story of how their three year old daughter had seen me go forward and had been so worried about what happened to me. Until they saw me in the court room, they had no idea that I had survived.

One of the most important things I learned was not to worry my head too much about double jeopardy. I still have some concerns, but after hearing the witnesses, I know in my heart that the fifteen years he served in a Pakistani jail were not enough. Whatever the legalities of his Pakistani trial, whatever the legalities of his release, whatever rules may have been broken in his recapture, he should not be at large in the world after what he did. I am not sure about solitary confinement underground, which I think is cruel and unusual punishment, but I am much less concerned that America acted wrongly in pursuing and arraigning him. That is, of course, difficult to fit into a comprehensive and coherent set of legal and moral principles; perhaps that's part of the psychological damage that Dr Main identified. I can believe contradictory things at the same time.

I was also greatly impressed with all the efforts put on by the Department of Justice. It would not be proper for them to spend public money in an extravagant way, but within those limits they did their very best to make sure that the survivors had the opportunity to come, to watch and listen, to speak if they wanted to. There were psychologists on hand to help if anyone found it too much; there was young Gregory running around dealing with everyone's tickets and expenses claims. The judge had declared that he wanted the victims to be heard: the plea bargain would not be a quiet deal between the State and the criminal, with the victims left out. The Department of Justice did their best to make that happen.

What I did not learn in America was why they started shooting. As far as I know, they have never explained it, and may even still deny that it happened.

Going home

After two days in court, many of the passengers and relatives ended up in the bar of the hotel for a final drink. Some of the hearing was replayed with commentary; there was some catching up on who lived where and how long it would take to get home; addresses were exchanged.

Sunshine told me that she had cut short her testimony. She was so angry that she was on the point of asking the judge if she could go over and slap Abbas. I thought Judge Sullivan would have been up for that: 160 years in Super Max and a slap from Sunshine. But maybe it would have been ruled out as cruel and unusual.

Kathy and I had an early plane to catch, and we were still jetlagged, so we left the others to go to bed. As I was walking away, Sunshine called after me, "Hey Mike!" I turned to look, and she raised her hand with her fingers pinched together as if she was holding something. "I've got your passport!", she laughed, with a wicked grin. This was in very poor taste. It was also one of the funniest things I've ever heard. I'm glad I'm not the only one to make bad jokes.

On the plane home, I watched a film which finished with the Beach Boys' song "God Only Knows" as the closing music. I found myself thinking of the flight attendants who had looked after me on the day, and how their lives had been torn apart in different ways, and my eyes watered. I hummed my own version: "God only knows where I'd be without you...".

THE END?

A never ending story

That is the end, but it is not the end. It is strange how sixteen hours of my life can still be so important after nearly twenty years. I hope the story has not grown in the telling, but somehow the telling of it has become part of the story, and for me it goes on.

*****

The story is not forgotten elsewhere, either. The US Department of Justice waits patiently for the four men in Pakistan to come out of jail. If they ever do, they can be sure that somewhere there will be some American agents looking out for them.

*****

America has also paid its tribute to the heroism at the heart of this book. On 21 April 2006 in Washington DC, the US Attorney General, Alberto Gonzales, presented a Special Courage Award to the cabin crew of PA 073 and to Viraf Daroga. This award is the highest award presented to crime victims by the United States Department of Justice. Neerja was singled out by India for posthumous recognition; it is good to see that the others are being recognised as well, if a little belatedly, while they are still alive. The citation for the award gives this summary:

The 16 flight attendants and the Pan Am Director for Pakistan, Viraf Daroga, showed incredible courage throughout the ordeal. Their combined efforts most likely saved the lives of more than 350 people and provided comfort and hope to the hostages during their captivity. The flight attendants risked their own lives to protect American citizens by hiding American passports from the hijackers, who were planning to execute Americans in support of the hijackers' demands. Director Viraf Daroga bravely stood within firing distance of the hijackers to negotiate, in an attempt to prevent passenger executions. During and immediately after the final deadly assault by the hijackers, the flight attendants heroically saved hundreds of lives by helping to open the emergency exits and to evacuate the passengers.

Flight attendant Neerja Bhanot lost her life during this act of heroism. Below the plane, Director Daroga assisted the injured passengers. For two days after the siege, the flight attendants cared for unaccompanied minor passengers, until they could be reunited with family. Director Daroga and several flight attendants courageously testified at the hijackers' trial in Pakistan, in the face of death threats. Several of the flight attendants and Director Daroga also provided emotional and powerful testimony during a sentencing proceeding for the lead hijacker, held in Washington, D.C. in May 2004.

*****

The hunt for the paymaster goes on, too. On 5 April 2006, a Washington DC law firm filed a lawsuit for damages in respect of the PA 073 hijacking. It is being brought on behalf of "one hundred seventy-six passengers, estates, and family members", and the claim is – pause for breath – $10 billion. That is… $10,000,000,000.

I find the numbers that American lawyers conjure up difficult to comprehend. I can't remember what their fee agreement amounts to, but any sort of percentage of that figure would be an extraordinary amount of money.

The problem in such a lawsuit seems to me to be the mixing together of appropriate punishment for the wrongdoers and appropriate compensation for the victims. I can quite see that an oil-rich country might properly have to pay (if it can be proved guilty) a huge sum of money to recognise the wrong and to express its remorse. It seems difficult to relate that to what the victims might be paid as compensation, but is there a more deserving recipient?

If the lawyers seriously believe that $10,000,000,000 is appropriate compensation for the class as whole, presumably they think that the victims should never have to work again. Split evenly between 176 people, that's (oops, I can't get that many zeroes on my calculator)… $56.8 million dollars (and change) each, subject to deduction of legal fees. If I had lost an arm or a leg, that would be a lot of money; if I had lost a wife or a daughter, it would be at the same time too much and not nearly enough. The lawyers can only represent loss in money, and money is altogether the wrong currency.

195

So I have put my name to this not in the hope of a share of the damages, but because the lawsuit will – I hope – force politicians to recall some recent history. The lawyers believe that Colonel Gadaffy was responsible. They think they can prove it, just as was proven with PA 103 at Lockerbie. Gadaffy has been an international pariah for years, but there has been some movement to bring him back into the fold. I do not like to see the British Prime Minister meeting with the man who paid for this act of murder. I would like it to be remembered; I do not think it should be quietly and conveniently forgotten.

If they prove it, and if Gadaffy pays, and if I am awarded any share of the money (three large ifs), then our local primary school may yet get the refurbishment that the British government won't pay for. It might have to change its name from "the Queen's School" to "the Colonel's School", though. We won't hold our breath.

Giving in to terrorists

And as for me, what have I learned from all this, and what has nearly twenty years of telling this story taught me? Over the years, I have spent too much time thinking about these events. Some things I am very clear about. As someone who has been a bargaining counter, I strongly support the view that terrorists' demands cannot be met, however extreme the pressure may be.

When the awful siege at Beslan in Russia was going on, some people expressed the view, "Surely we have to give in because they have taken children hostage". This may get these children out on this occasion, but it sends out a powerful message to people with demands: *if you take children hostage, you will get more than if you take adults hostage. If you threaten to do something really horrible, we will give you what you want.* Unfortunately, there will always be some who will "stop at nothing" to get what they want; enough of them to create a great deal of grief. It is impossible to guard against them everywhere, all the time. If they know they will not have their demands met, in any circumstances whatever, it slightly reduces their incentive to threaten ghastly things.

That's the long-term policy, but it has to be applied in short-term crises. Giving in to an immediate demand may seem tempting to put off a deadline, but it's unlikely to improve the situation. Take the pressure that Abbas was willing to exert on the negotiators by refusing treatment to a sick passenger. If you have nearly four hundred hostages, you need to get the whole thing done before you have to sleep. He wanted to turn the screw on the negotiators, and having a victim moaning and groaning by the radio would be helpful. "If you give us a pilot, we will let this person off." Of course, it makes no sense – you get this person off, and then you say goodbye to the other three hundred and eighty who are on their way to God knows where. But it's not easy for the negotiators to keep to that hard, logical, obvious conclusion when they are presented with the immediate suffering of one person.

The popular media do not help us to confront these realities. I've already described the ridiculous scene with the grenade-man in the nameless TV movie about a hijack. Far more dangerous is the subversive message in *Air Force One*, a much better film and a very popular one. I don't want to give away too much of the plot to anyone who hasn't seen it, but it should certainly carry a government health warning. The terrorists want to spring some evil rebel warlord from jail in Russia, where he has been rightly imprisoned after due process of law. They have taken Air Force One and are holding various members of the US President's family hostage. The leader threatens to kill the President's teenage daughter. As a result, the Vice-President gives in to his demands.

That is bad enough – back to the subliminal suggestion, "take our children, then we'll give in" – but what I found worse was the portrayal of the opposing argument, put forward by some minor character (maybe the Secretary of State or Secretary for Defence). He reasons that we should not allow the warlord out, possibly leading to the deaths of many, many other people, in order to save this one child now. He is portrayed as wrong, inhuman, callous. I suppose all those many other people are anonymous Russians in the future, and the teenager is a cute American girl in immediate peril.

I hope that the real Vice-President would see it differently. I also hope it is harder for terrorists to get on board Air Force One than it appears to be in the film!

Hearts and minds

The sad and awkward truth is that terrorism has worked very well to get certain causes up the political agenda. Even where the cause has minimal popular support – such as the Red Army Factions and other communist extremists in the 1970s – terrorism put something on the agenda which would not have been there at all. Where there is a genuine grievance, often with an insoluble underlying problem and a long history of conflict, it has helped to bring politicians to the negotiating table – however much they may protest that they do not negotiate with terrorists – when they might otherwise have been able to carry on ignoring the issue. In my view, this has applied to Irish Republican terrorism and Palestinian terrorism. In the short term, and to that limited extent, it "works", and that is a very uncomfortable fact for democracies to deal with.

However, it doesn't seem to get anywhere after that. It can't bring peace, because it deepens wounds which need to be healed, and increases fear where trust is needed. There will be tit for tat and an eye for an eye, and an ongoing cycle of violence without end, while the grievance continues unresolved. Both sides become increasingly entrenched behind the defences they put up against terror attacks and retaliation.

Do people like Abbas have any notion of all that? They may believe that they really will achieve the immediate goal – they really will spring some convicted terrorists from jail in Cyprus. Or they may not particularly care: they have been persuaded that what they are doing is "for the cause", and if they die doing it, they will go straight to heaven to be waited on by seventy virgins in a non-sensual manner (some might think that this would be hell rather than heaven, but it can be hard to put yourself into the mind of another person).

The people above Abbas in the terrorist hierarchy have a good understanding of what the mission is actually about. The mission, the impact, is the end in itself. They know that terrorism will not bring peace. Provocation of a reaction, so that more and more people will become involved, seems to be one of the aims of terrorist groups. It is easy to see the short-term result: send four Muslim suicide bombers onto the London Underground; the great majority of Muslims are utterly horrified, but then unjustified attacks by white people on uninvolved Muslims increase dramatically; even moderate Muslims are driven to the barricades. It is a perverse way of recruiting support, by increasing the level of general hatred.

The long-term objective of the terrorists is to force the legitimate government to make political concessions. Whatever else we feel about it, terrorism is rational (even if the low-grade terrorists may not be), and our political response needs to be rational as well. Conducting a war on terror by trying to kill all the terrorists individually seems completely futile – every one you kill will be represented as a martyr and will help to recruit ten more. There's a place for killing terrorists, but it won't work on its own.

I have said that I felt sorry for Abbas, maybe because I was foolishly accepting his short speech at face value. I didn't feel so sorry for Ali, because he was always nasty – but I thought I could *understand* him. For years, I had a vision of this man growing up somewhere in the Middle East – maybe in a refugee camp in the Lebanon – and being told constantly that the reason for all the misery in his life is his list of "rich people". He had probably never met a real Spanish person, but he hated them all, as he told us. It's easy to say that hijackers and suicide bombers are all evil, but there is a problem – who is there to tell this young man the truth? How can you stop the recruiters feeding stories to people like Ali? Until we can think of a way, denouncing Ali as evil gets us nowhere. The recruiters are undoubtedly evil. The Alis of this world are misguided.

When the bombs exploded in London on 7 July 2005, I had to reconsider my view: these recruits grew up in Yorkshire and Buckinghamshire, not in a refugee camp. They had every opportunity to see that suicide bombing was a cruel, futile and evil act that would change nothing and would be an affront to their religion. Still they went ahead. It is a shock, but it has confirmed my view of Ali – if it was possible to indoctrinate these people, how much easier was it to do the same to Ali?

The War on Terror

This is the fundamental issue for the "war on terror": if the actions of the American and British governments make it easier to recruit terrorists, then those actions are likely to be counter-productive.

I am not alone in thinking that we are not waging the "war on terror" very effectively. The arguments are fairly well established, and few people will change their views based on what I write here – so I will be brief. The big problem with fighting terrorists is that they are hard to find. As a result, you spend a lot of time, money and effort looking for them and perhaps not achieving very much – or not appearing to achieve very much. That looks bad, so there is an enormous temptation to do something much more visible, which may not actually be very effective in your war on terror.

It's likely that the removal of the Taliban and the denial of Afghanistan to Al-Qaeda was a good thing in the war on terror. It probably did make the world a safer place, at least for a while. It's much less clear that the second Iraq war had much to do with terrorism, or will make the world safer. I am not going to argue that it was wrong to invade Iraq. It may have been a good thing, it may have been a just war, it may have removed an awful dictator; but one reason given was that it was part of a war on terror, and it almost certainly didn't advance that.

A war on terror can only finally be won by reducing the number of people who are tempted to use it. That involves working on the reasons that people take it up – winning over hearts and minds. Anything that provides a recruiting call to those who hate us is a losing move in the war on terror.

One example was much on our minds during the sentencing proceeding of May 2004, because it was on the news every night: the maltreatment of Iraqi prisoners in the Abu Graibh prison by US soldiers. I doubt that the American administration planned it or ordered it; but the administration should have been making absolutely sure that no such thing could ever happen. They needed to prove to the potential terror recruits that American justice was fair and honest; many would not believe it anyway, but to prove the opposite so graphically was something that should not have been remotely possible.

I don't know whether it will ever be possible to undo the damage that the war has done to the prospect of peace between westerners – in particular, Americans and Britons – and Muslims. There are plenty of people who are prepared to be friendly with each other, but plenty who are not. The war on terror appears bent on finding and killing the terrorists one by one. For every one you kill, there will be five new recruits. I'm not sentimental about killing terrorists, but let's not pretend this will win the war. It just won't work. The bigger, more difficult policy issues lie elsewhere, and I fear that they will be left for a new generation of political leaders to tackle.

Closure

Many people talk about "closure" as something that trauma victims need to achieve in order to get on with the rest of their lives. I am not sure whether it was a common expression when I went to see Dr Main, but I am sure he would have recognised the concept: I went to Pakistan to achieve closure of the grieving process for my brother's death. I stood at the bottom of the mountain and said goodbye, and that would enable me to move on. To move on to Karachi...

Many people talked about the possibility of closure for the victims of the hijacking while we were in Washington. The punishment of the criminal is supposed to be some comfort to the people who suffered at his hands. There is something about the finality of the Super Max door shutting on Safarini that might seem to open a new chapter for the victims. I doubt if it works like that. If someone has been looking for closure for 18 years, they are unlikely to achieve it from watching one of the hijackers led away to the cells. He's still alive; the other terrorists are still in Pakistan; the injuries and the memories remain; the dead are still dead. There is no finality.

I believe that closure, in the sense of being able to move on and enjoy a life free of the bitterness of the hijack, can only come from inside the person. The knowledge that the hijackers are being punished may help, but not much. I think the bitterness comes from within, as well – as long as the victim broods on the horror, it will remain horrible, and the status of "victim" continues.

It wasn't the most popular sentiment in the courtroom, but I think the priest was right: peace comes from forgiveness. That was easy for me: I had no physical injury, I lost no loved ones, I determined to forgive them before the hijack was even over. Afterwards, I felt nothing but the joy of a new life given back to me to make the most of. I could forgive them for myself, and put all to rest inside me. Even if they had crippled me, at least it would be within my power to forgive them for that. But if they had killed my father, my wife, my sister, my daughter… it would be impossible to put it to rest. That is the hardest thing of all, I think – for those who were not there, but whose loved ones suffered, the pain is possibly greater and longer-lasting than for those who were actually present.

Forgiveness is also not a popular political agenda: it seems weak. A president is expected to inflict retaliation for his people's suffering on the perpetrators or, if they can't be found, on someone who might be connected with them. So the cycle of violence continues. I can't see an answer to that, until something remarkable happens that makes people face up to the need for reconciliation. The kind of entrenched conflict that led to this hijacking requires both sides to want peace and both sides to make concessions.

Still, miracles sometimes happen. I've known that every day since 5 September 1986.

APPENDICES

Further reading

Catherine Hill, who was horribly injured at the end of the hijack, has told her story – mainly about getting her life back afterwards – in "Dancing in the Sea" (Mainstream Publishing, ISBN 1-84018-877-4). My experience is a bit of a picnic in comparison. If you read her book, you might suspect that I have made the whole thing up, because she calls me "Peter George". She took a similar decision to mine about not wanting to tell other people's stories. But it really was me.

The full story of Pete's last expedition is beautifully told by Greg Child in "Thin Air" (Patrick Stephens, ISBN 1-85260-045-4), and the chapter "On Broad Peak" in "Mixed Emotions" (The Mountaineers, ISBN 0-89886-363-5) is a shorter account of their last climb together. I read the story of Pete's death in 1988 after it was published, and have never managed to read it again since.

The summer of 1986 was full of drama on the Baltoro Glacier, with 13 deaths on K2 while we were camped at Urdukas. The British expedition leader, Al Rouse, was the patron of our expedition and one of the casualties. Jim Curran's book "K2: Triumph and Tragedy" (Hodder & Stoughton, ISBN 0-340-41526-6) tells that story. He is an old friend of Pete's – the cine-cameras I took to Pakistan were his.

One last book: "Just for the love of it" by Cathy O'Dowd, "the first woman to climb Everest from both sides" (Free to Decide, ISBN 0-620-24782-7). I was amazed to find, idly Googling my own name one day "as you do", the poem that I read out to Pete at the foot of Broad Peak reproduced in the website of a famous South African climber, and also printed in her book about her mountaineering career. The poem acquired a life of its own: the 1987 Pete Thexton Memorial Expedition to South America was also struck by tragedy when two of the medical student climbers fell to their deaths. My poem for Pete was printed in the order of service for their memorial. Someone must have taken it home and pinned it up, because Cathy O'Dowd saw it on the wall of a London flat she lived in during 1992, and she learned it by heart, not knowing who I was or anything about the "Pete" in the title.

For Pete, 1983

Cathy O'Dowd recited this poem – or part of it – for her friend Bruce
Herrod who died on Everest in 1996, and she says it has meant a lot to
her. So I'll put it in here as well.

My family is four, but one lies cold,
Returns not from the hills that were his life –
And death; now only lives in hearts that grieve,
And in wild spirits who look up with him.
If I could live to see a thousand years,
The pride and memory and pain live with me;
A gap so wide, but not a bitterness,
For you could not have lived in any other way.

You stood above me, held me on the rope,
And lifted me yourself when I would fall.
You cursed me for my fear, I you for seeing it –
When could I be as safe as in your hands?
How can a man so strong yield up his life?
You were so full of it. It burned in you,
Full-filled your unforgiving thirty years
With headlong centuries of distance run.

The mountains are not mindful of mankind.
Immune to siege, resisting all intrusion,
They tolerate in their eternity
The climber's fleeting insignificance.
And yet, accepting you as one belonging,
They hold you now, in death as life at home;
At home in cold, steep, hostile places,
Until the glacier rolls into the sea.

I hear you calling me, from your white silence –
A memory of a time including you,
You speak, although my world includes you not –
For time has hardly touched your memory.
Are these the sane, ten million plastic souls
Who run so lonely on their daily round?
Are they so mad, who climb the peaks and die?
What loss is life, to one who finds himself?

I see you still, in dreams and strangers' faces,
In some expressions of my morning mirror;
But cannot reach you in your solitude,
Nor breathe the same thin air that laid you down.
You grow not old, as I, being left, grow old.
I age, wane weary, am condemned by years;
You, thirty still, become my younger brother,
Lie frozen in the beauty of your strength.

I never will again hold back on love:
Love's object may not stay to share tomorrow –
Life, like a welcome guest, too soon departing.
I would give all my world to have you back,
Remember you not in a photograph
But in your smiling eyes and wild ideal.
And yet, I would not pay a price too high:
I would not think of asking you to change.

And though your rope is cut, and worlds have fallen,
And though the pain will grip me through the years,
If you were with me now, I still would help,
Encourage you to reach for mountain tops –
Would watch you strive for where you should not go.
And you would go again, and die again,
And I would cry; but cry how much the more
If you should ever cease to be yourself.

The 1983 expedition

I have a poster on my wall, signed by all the nine members of Pete's 1983 expedition: by the end of the 1980s, four of them – Pete, Don Whillans, Roger Baxter-Jones, and Al Rouse – were dead, and another – Andy Parkin – had suffered horrific injuries in a fall. Only Whillans had managed to die in his bed. But the rest of them seem to be cheating the law of averages: Doug Scott, Greg Child, Jean Afanasieff, and Steve Sustad are all still going, and Andy Parkin has rebuilt himself as both a climber and a painter.

Breakfast Time

Here is my full interview with Nick Ross, BBC Breakfast Time, 8 September 1986.

NR   Good morning. You must have been enormously relieved to get home last night. You got in, what, 8 o'clock last night. Did you get any sleep?

MT   Yes, there were a few phone calls coming in late last night, I got to sleep about 11 I suppose. First good night's sleep I've had, I suppose, since the hijack.

NR   And it really was a good night's sleep – apart from the fact that you had to get up for Breakfast Time – no nightmares?

MT   No, nothing at all, it was OK.

NR   Describe what happened when the hijack first started. What was your first realisation that it was going on?

MT   Well, I had just got on the plane and I had put my bags down on my seat and was getting a book out or something, and I suddenly saw this man with a pistol struggling with an air stewardess in the second doorway, and I just stood there looking at it and thinking, what's going on here? It's the sort of thing you think happens to other people, I couldn't work it out.

NR   The stewardess was actually struggling – was she trying to disarm him, trying to block him?

MT   Yes, I think she had the telephone in her hand, I think she might have been trying to warn the aircrew or something like that. Then I turned round and there was a man in the front doorway who was dressed as a security guard, and I thought ah, security have arrived, it's all right. Then he was telling the stewardess to close the door and everyone to get down, this is a hijack. I realised that perhaps he wasn't what he was supposed to be.

NR   He said that in English?

MT   Yes, he was telling people to get down, in English.

NR   How does the body react to that? Did you feel your heartbeat going up? What was your own reaction?

MT   It's very difficult to remember exactly what was going through my mind – you did what he said, you got down. And there was a burst of gunfire at that stage. I think he was firing out of the plane, but you didn't really stop to look which way he was pointing.

NR   Jumbo jets are pretty big things, but because you'd just got on, you were pretty close to where all this was going on, were you?

MT   Yes, I was right up at the front.

NR   Now the next thing, as I understand it, was that passports were collected. Tell me about what happened.

MT   After about an hour and a half – we'd actually been sitting with our hands on our heads and our heads down for most of that time – we'd actually been moved back into the main section of the plane and told to sit very still or we'd get shot –

NR   Was everybody still, then? There must have been lots of kids, what was the noise like?

MT   There was no noise, everyone was very quiet.

NR   Including the little children?

MT   Including the little children. There'd be occasional crying, but they were very good all day and the passengers as a whole were very calm. But then the stewardess said we should hold up our passports in one hand, and I thought for a moment about whether I could actually hide it, because I thought a British passport was not a great thing to hand in – but there were a few Americans about, and I thought, you know, they'll be in front of us. I held it up and the stewardess came round with a bag and she collected it and then she went back to the front of the plane. And after probably another ten minutes the stewardess came on the intercom again and said would Mr Michael John please come to the front of the plane. That's my first two names, and I thought, Oh my God, and then she said, Will Mr Michael John Thexton please come to the front of the plane, and I thought, again, can I hide under the seat here somewhere? But by that stage they were looking for me, they would come and find me. There isn't much place to hide on a jumbo jet. And so I had to go up to the front.

NR   What did you feel as you walked towards the front?

MT   Well, I was absolutely terrified. I mean, I was just wondering, why me, why am I on this plane, all those sorts of things.

NR   You couldn't have known at this stage that the flight crew had actually escaped down a rope from a hatch in the top of the cockpit.

MT   Well, I had suspected it because one of the first announcements that they got the stewardess to make was can anyone operate the cockpit radio. So we presumed from that the people who could operate the cockpit radio had either died or gone, and I remember thinking, what a relief, we're probably not going to fly anywhere.

NR   You thought at the time that it was a good thing that they'd got out?

MT   Yes, absolutely.

NR   So you arrived at the front of this immobilised plane. You met the hijackers, did you?

MT   Yes.

NR   What were they like?

MT   Well, the leader of the hijackers, he was a tall man, quite good-looking. He'd taken his shirt off at this stage, so he was standing there just in his trousers. And he was quite calm, very polite. At times he was apologetic – I've been told that's a psychological tactic, to get you sympathetic to them, but he was always very considerate to me while I was at the front of the plane... apart from the fact that he had a gun on me most of the time.

NR   And was he brandishing the gun – did he look as if he was going to shoot you? Did he say anything to you?

MT   Yes, well, he asked me a couple of questions. He asked me if I was a soldier – he asked me if I had a gun, which I thought was quite funny… well, in a sort of way. Then he told me to kneel down by the door, then he got the stewardess, who had a megaphone, to speak out of the door to people on the tarmac and he said: tell them that if there are any police near, or if any US soldiers arrive, we will shoot one person immediately – which I took to be me.

NR   Now, tell us how it ended. What was your first recognition that something was happening, something that fundamental?

MT   I was actually asleep at the front of the plane. I had been up there for thirteen hours with very little to do, I couldn't talk to anybody really. There were some air stewardesses there, but I felt so conspicuous that I couldn't do anything at all. So I was asleep and suddenly one of the hijackers kicked my feet and said move, move. And I think the lights had gone down, the main lights had gone off and the emergency lights had come on, and I got up and stumbled back down the plane, I was not quite working out what was going on, but it was obvious that something was happening because I'd been moved. And I went and found a spare seat, near one of the wing exits, because I thought that looked a pretty good place to get down. And then the emergency lights got dimmer as well, and as far as I can remember they actually went out, and it was very dark. And suddenly there was shooting and bangs, and we all got down in our seats.

NR   Including you…

MT   Yes, including me. Right down on the floor.

NR   How did you get out?

MT   Well, when there was a moment, and I could get my head up, I could see light coming in round one of the wing exits where obviously a passenger was opening the door, so I said to the person next to me, go on, they're opening the doors, let's get out of this plane, and he said, no, get down, get down, but I said no, come on, so I sort of pushed him out and we made our way to the exit behind us, and jumped out on the wing, and I jumped down onto the tarmac.

NR   Was shooting going on behind you?

MT   Yes, there was still – it was sporadic, it wasn't continuous, but there was still shooting in the plane when I was getting down on the tarmac.

NR   It must have been an extraordinary feeling getting out of this plane. Were you frightened the whole time that bullets were going to come...?

MT   Well, one of the worst things was that, because they had been dressed as security guards, you didn't know who to trust. For some of the day, we were thinking that this was some sort of revolution going on, so some of us ran and hid in a building, and waited for everything to die down, hoping that the first policeman to arrive was a real policeman, and not one of their accomplices.

NR   Well, Mike, we all delighted and relieved that you got back, not just in such good physical shape, but so well psychologically as well. Thank you very much for retelling your experiences. And I hope that in a way it's cathartic and helps to tell the story rather than dredging it all up again.

MT   Yes, I think it's probably a good thing.

Thought for the Day

Here is what I said for "Thought for the Day" on TV-AM, Sunday 14 September 1986:

Good morning. Nine days ago, I was on the hijacked aeroplane at Karachi airport. Because of my British passport, the terrorists singled me out, and I had to wait at the front of the plane in case they needed someone to shoot to emphasise one of their demands. Mercifully, it's not a situation which happens to many people, or very often, but I've been asked to say how I coped.

I was quite convinced that, at some point of the day, they would shoot someone, and it would most likely be me. I started off by being terrified, obviously. I had thought that we would be all right if everyone kept calm and I kept my head down, but here I was on my own, with the terrorist leader saying that he would shoot a passenger if his demands weren't met. I knew quite well that the authorities couldn't give in, and when it happens to someone else, I'm ready to say that the authorities shouldn't give in.

I was told to kneel behind the closed door, and I couldn't think of any possible way to escape. When I tried to plead with the terrorist, he just waved his hand as if to say, I haven't any time for that. So I was left to my own thoughts. I started by praying, and that's something I hadn't done for a long time. The trouble was that I felt such a hypocrite. If you don't think praying is going to help normally, then why should it help now? But I made all sorts of promises, which one way or another I suppose I'll keep, because my prayer was answered. I don't know whether it was anything to do with what I said, but a promise is a promise.

I also felt that it was so completely inadequate. When you are faced with a man holding a gun, then there is no price that you can possibly put on your own life. Anything you can do or promise seems trivial in comparison.

So, I was still very frightened. I was mainly feeling sorry for my family, who had already lost one son and brother in the mountains in Pakistan, and I wasn't sure that they could cope with another grief. So

I asked one of the stewardesses to pass a message to them if I was shot: tell my family I love them very much. That made me feel a bit better, so I tried to think of all the people who I would miss, and who would miss me. I pictured them all in my mind. I was still sure that they would kill me, so it was like saying goodbye. And it calmed me down.

Then I tried to think of all the people I might have argued with, or had a grudge against, or might have parted from on bad terms. I've heard it said, "Never go to sleep on a quarrel", and somehow I felt that I didn't want to die with any hatred in my heart. And that brought me eventually to the man with the gun. It never actually came to it, but while I was on my knees, I thought I was actually prepared to shake his hand and forgive him. After that, I didn't really feel so bad at all, and I was able just to sit and wait to see what happened.

I think that I must have used a lifetime's worth of luck getting out of the plane. There are all sorts of reasons why I should have been one of the people who was killed or injured. And because I'm all right, I don't really think that it's up to me now to forgive or condemn the terrorists, because in the end they didn't really do anything to me. If I'd lost a leg, I might well hate them forever. So I can't now say how I feel towards them. All I can say, is that to be given a second life when you have said goodbye to the first one is the most extraordinary feeling, and I'll really try to make the most of it.

Sentencing proceeding

Here is the first part of my address to the Federal Court at the Sentencing Proceeding, 12 May 2004. The conclusion – my feelings about the effect on me afterwards – are in the main story on pages 177 and 178.

My name is Michael Thexton, from England. I was 27 in 1986. I was in Pakistan for two months on a mountaineering expedition in the Karakoram Himalayas in the north of that country. The expedition was held in memory of my brother Peter, who died of altitude sickness there in 1983, and he is buried high in the mountains. Although I am not a mountaineer, I went along with the other members of the expedition to stand at the foot of the mountain and say goodbye to my brother.

Coming out of the mountains, I received some mail saying that I was expected back at work sooner than I had thought, and I used this as an excuse to rearrange my flight. In reality, I just wanted to get home: I had been to the mountain and said goodbye to my brother, and I really wanted to see the rest of my family as soon as possible. I was so keen to get back that, for the only time in my life so far, I stretched my funds to buy a business class ticket, because no other earlier flights were available.

I was a curious sight in the First and Business class departure lounge at Karachi airport – I had a long beard, long hair, deep suntan, and about 35 pounds less weight than I am carrying today. In the days immediately afterwards, some people said that the hijack must have been dreadful because of the way that I looked, but really that was the two months beforehand in the mountains.

I boarded the plane by the port forward door, and I was directed to a seat a few rows back, on that aisle. I saw the first hijacker while I was standing by my seat getting ready to stow my hand luggage – a man was struggling with a stewardess in the second doorway. A moment later a man dressed as a security guard and armed with a rifle appeared in the doorway by which I had just entered, and he ordered the stewardess to close the door.

At first I thought that this was a domestic Pakistani disturbance happening on the surface, and the security guard was protecting us, but soon someone said, "This is a hijack, put your hands in the air", and I had the awful sinking realisation that this could be my problem. Very soon the first and business class passengers were herded back to the front cabin of the economy section, and some went on down the plane. I found a seat on the port aisle. Others sat on the floor.

We sat with our hands in the air. I want to say two things about that. Afterwards, the journalists eagerly asked, "Did they beat you?" – and they seemed a bit disappointed when I said, "No, but they made us sit with our hands in the air". For how long, I don't know. There are many people here who will understand that it gets pretty hard quite quickly. The drawn-out discomfort, combined with acute fear, is not much short of a beating. We were lucky – we were allowed to lower our hands after a while, and sitting on the hard floor lasted no more than about 16 hours. But in a way it could be worse than a beating – at least if you have taken a beating, it's easier to realise how tough it was. If you don't get beaten up, but you end up physically fouling yourself, or you have a mental breakdown, you might come out thinking that you have failed somehow, that it's your fault. But you have been put in an intolerable position, and it is absolutely his fault, it's not your fault at all.

The other thing is that I was terrorised. The word terrorism is used so much to describe a global news issue that I think people forget what it means, individually and in detail. For myself, I was deprived of the capacity for rational thought. I was convinced that there was a man with a gun right behind me watching my every move. For most of the day, they had just two people guarding more than 350, many of whom they couldn't even see. But they could probably have left the plane at this point and gone to have breakfast, and if they'd come back half an hour later, I at least would still have been sitting with my hands in the air.

I tried to get a grip of myself, and I told myself that people survive hijacks. I should try to remain inconspicuous, do what I was told, and I would be all right. I looked at the people sitting next to me, a man and his wife, who looked to me as if they were American, and possibly

215

Jewish as well. And I thought, "They are in front of me". It was a brutal thing to think – I hope it was not just me, looking around for someone who was in a worse position than themselves.

I sank down in my seat to be out of the way, and once we were allowed to lower our hands I felt pretty well invisible and reasonably safe. I was just a few rows behind where Rajesh Kumar was taken from, but I did not see him go, and I did not hear him shot. I was trying to hide from everything that was going on, I think.

Then came the call for passports, and I should have ignored it, but I felt that I had to obey orders. So I handed mine in, still thinking that the Americans would be in front, not reckoning with the ingenuity and great bravery of the stewardess making the collection. I suppose the British were the third choice target behind Israelis and Americans, and mine was one of only a handful of British passports with white faces in the pile.

So the call came for passenger Michael John to come forward, then Michael John Thexton, and I knew that they wanted to shoot me. I could not understand it. I knew I could not hide from them, so I stood up – I am afraid that I uttered an obscenity at this point – and went forward, past one gunman standing at the front row of the economy class. By the front port door, where I had entered earlier, there were four stewardesses in two rows of seats, and the security guard, now stripped to the waist with a white band showing above his belt, and with his Kalashnikov rifle across his chest, holding my passport.

He asked me a few questions – "Are you a soldier?" "No, I'm a teacher." "Do you have a gun?" I just laughed, it was so ridiculous. "No, you've got all the guns around here." Then he told me to kneel in the space behind the door, which was open a crack. One of the stewardesses relayed a message by megaphone to someone below the nose of the plane. I now know that this man was Viraf Daroga. "If anyone comes near the plane, if any US troops come near the plane, we will kill one body immediately." One body, that was what I was to him. "I have bombers on board, and all my men are commandos."

Mr Daroga replied that there was a ground crew member on board who could operate the cockpit radio, and this man – Meherjee Kharas –

216

was called forward. I now understand that he was in a way traded for me, to stop Safarini shooting me, and I am saddened to know that he died. The door was closed. I spent the next 10 hours or so kneeling, sitting and lying on the floor behind that closed door, waiting for them to make a demand that would not be met, when I would be shot. I was absolutely certain that this would happen. I did not know, as the stewardesses did, that it had already happened to Rajesh Kumar: as far as I knew, I would be the first.

I will tell you a few things about that time. I felt awful, but mainly for my parents and sisters, who had already lost one son and brother in Pakistan, and now would lose the other. I at least had been able to say goodbye to my brother. So I said goodbye in my mind to my family and friends. Today, when I have a wife and two daughters, I do not think I could do that – it would tear me to pieces to think that I would never see them again, and I would not be able to say goodbye in person. I think that I was very fortunate to be travelling alone on that day.

Apart from saying goodbye, I said prayers, and I made promises to be kept in the unlikely event of a miracle that would lead to my survival. I kept those promises, because I do not want to have to argue with St Peter that I short-changed the Almighty for my life. I made my peace with God, and in my mind I made my peace with these men. I did not want to die angry or frightened. I made up my mind to forgive them.

Throughout that time, I was probably kept sane by the kindness of the flight attendants, several of them here today, and I thank them. But I think that they knew as well as I did that I was a dead man.

I had a very little conversation with the leader. At one point the stewardesses were down the plane serving drinks and he sat opposite me. I would not speak unless spoken to, but he said, "Are you married?" I replied, "No, I have a girlfriend". "Oh. I am sorry about this. I do not like this fighting, this killing. I would like to go out dancing, go out drinking, go out with women. But the Americans and Israelis have stolen my country, and without my country, these things are no good." "Oh, so you're Palestinian, then?" "Yes, Palestinian."

217

I don't know why he said this to me. Maybe he was playing me for a sucker. I have to say I felt sorry for him. I felt that he was perhaps not just a madman doing this because he liked it, but maybe he really did believe it would help a cause he really believed to be just. But how sad that is, to carry on the circle of killing, on and on, an unjust act diminishing the justice of the cause and reducing the likelihood of a proper peaceful settlement.

Apart from that, they never gave me any indication of what they wanted. They treated us as nothing more than trading stock, to be bargained with or disposed of.

Of the rest of the day, I will only say that some time later, I woke up from a doze to see Neerja* and another stewardess opening a small hatch in the floor below the spiral staircase. The leader came clattering down the stairs. "What are you doing?" "We have a sick passenger, we have found a doctor, we are getting out the medical equipment." He just said, "Put it back". Neerja said, "But we need the medical equipment for the sick passenger." He said again to put it back. At that she stood up to him and waved a finger in his face, and said angrily, "You are a very bad man. These people have done nothing to you. You must let us take the medical equipment for the sick passenger." He was quite calm, but he insisted that they put it back. Neerja had to go and explain, and I remember thinking, "That's funny, he's been quite reasonable all day, why won't he let them have the medical equipment?" Quite reasonable – my view had become so distorted that I was prepared to think of his lack of direct violence towards me as quite reasonable.

It took me years to realise that he could be a reasonable man driven to brutality in his cause, or he could be a brutal man pretending to be reasonable when it suited him, and I would not be able to tell the difference. But either way, a sick passenger moaning and groaning would probably be quite a good lever in the negotiations on the radio.

I was woken again by one of the others kicking my feet and telling me to move back down the plane. I did so, noticing it was hotter and darker. I found an empty window seat just forward of the port wing. In the pause that followed the first burst of shooting, I escaped though the exit there onto the wing, jumped to the ground – lucky to be 35 pounds underweight, very fit, and still wearing my mountaineering boots – and ran away.

* I had always assumed that Neerja was the flight attendant who argued with Abbas about the medical equipment, because she was the senior purser and was quite likely to have been asked to find a doctor. However, I have not been able to confirm this for sure – sadly, of course, Neerja herself is unable to tell her story. In telling the story in this book, I have tried to stick only to things that I can confirm for sure, so I have not given that brave woman a name. I have asked several of the surviving flight attendants if it was them, and the fact that they say it was not may mean that it was indeed Neerja, but I have not asked everyone. Fortunately, this little detail was not relevant to the court's proceedings.

The lawsuit against Libya

This is the press release put out by Crowell & Moring to explain the lawsuit filed on 5 April 2006:

Washington, D.C. – April 5, 2006: One hundred seventy-six passengers, estates, and family members who were victims of the September 5, 1986 terrorist hijacking of Pan Am Flight 73 in Karachi, Pakistan filed suit today against Libya and the individuals convicted of launching the attack. The Pan Am 73 terrorist attack killed 20 passengers and crew and severely injured more than 100 of the 380 persons on board.

The lawsuit was filed by the law firm Crowell & Moring LLP in the U.S. District Court for the District of Columbia, and seeks $10 billion in compensatory damages, as well as unspecified punitive damages, from Libya, its long-time leader, Muammar Qadhafi, and the five convicted terrorists, all of whom were members of the notorious terrorist group Abu Nidal Organization (ANO). Coming together from across the globe, the victims and family members who brought suit include the estates of 13 people murdered in the attack, 32 of their family members, and 131 other passengers and crew.

The hijackers had intended to fly the jumbo jet to Israel and crash it into the city of Tel Aviv. However, the pilots were alerted to the attack by the crew, and were able to escape by climbing out of the cockpit using emergency ropes. Without pilots, the hijackers could not get the aircraft off the ground.

The result was a terrifying 16 hour drama of killings, torture, and bravery. When the hijackers demanded that all passengers produce their passports, several crew members hid the passports of the Americans to protect those passengers who were the immediate targets. During the tense hours inside the large aircraft, the terrorists shot and killed an American citizen, heaved his body out of the plane's door onto the tarmac, and threatened to kill another passenger every ten minutes if their demands were not met. As the aircraft's power failed and the lights went out, the hijackers recited a martyrdom prayer, opened fire on the passengers with automatic weapons at point blank range, and threw hand grenades into the tightly packed group. In addition to the 20 passengers and crew who were killed, many more were severely maimed, blinded, or disfigured by bullets, grenades, and shrapnel. Several victims broke their legs and arms when they hit the tarmac after jumping from the doors to escape the bullets and explosives.

The five hijackers were convicted by the Pakistani courts for their roles in the attack. The leader of the hijackers on the plane, Zaid Safarini, was captured by the FBI when he was released from prison in Pakistan, and was brought to the United States for trial. On December 16, 2003, Safarini pled guilty in Washington, D.C. federal district court and was sentenced to three consecutive life sentences plus 25 years, which he is serving in a Colorado federal prison. The four other terrorists remain in Pakistani jails, and the United States has attempted to extradite them for prosecution in Washington, D.C. The United States government has publicly stated that Libya provided ANO with material support for the hijacking and also ordered the attack as part of its terrorist campaign against American, European, and Israeli interests.

Surviving passenger Jay Grantier, a resident of the state of Washington, said, "This was an attack on America. The terrorists murdered their first victim because he was an American, and when they ordered the cabin crew to collect all our passports, it was pretty obvious that they intended to kill more of us in the hours to come."

California resident and surviving passenger Nikita Patel was traveling from India to New York with her father, Surendra, on Pan Am Flight 73 when it was hijacked. Both were American citizens; Nikita was only 12 years old and Surendra had just celebrated his 50th birthday. The ANO hijackers shot Surendra as Nikita and her sister sat in the seats next to him. Surendra left behind a wife and three children. "I have had to live with the grief that comes from losing my father. I was too young to fight back then, but I can fight now. We can fight for justice that is long overdue for the hundreds of people whose lives were forever changed by this unthinkable crime," said Patel.

"Victims of terrorism have rights, and the courts will hold responsible the guilty parties who otherwise might believe there is no consequence for their heinous crimes," said Stuart Newberger, the victims' lead attorney and a senior partner at the international law firm Crowell & Moring. "The victims who filed this lawsuit today have been waiting for 20 years, and they have faith that justice will ultimately prevail."

Seetharamiah Krishnaswamy was traveling with his wife on Pan Am Flight 73 when it was hijacked. He and his wife were traveling to the United States to attend the wedding of one of their daughters. Krishnaswamy was murdered, leaving behind a wife and four children. His son, Dr. Prabhat Krishnaswamy, an Ohio resident, said "It was only after the Safarini sentencing in 2004 that the victims uncovered Libya's role in this attack. We formed a unified group determined to seek the truth behind this hijacking and hold Libya accountable." Recently, the U.S. Department of Justice recognized Dr. Krishnaswamy with a prestigious award for his "courage, perseverance, and commitment in seeking justice" on behalf of the Pan Am 73 families. Krishnaswamy added, " Libya has attempted to get off the list of state sponsors of terrorism and earn some sort of legitimate place in the world. But the victims remember. We are still here, and we are not standing down until we achieve justice. We owe this to the memory of the 20 innocent people who were murdered that day."